# FREUD
## *A Man of His Century*

# FREUD

# A Man of

# His Century

**GUNNAR BRANDELL**
*Professor of the History of Literature*
*Uppsala University*

TRANSLATED BY
**IAIN WHITE**

**HARVESTER PRESS • SUSSEX**
**HUMANITIES PRESS • NEW JERSEY**

First published in Great Britain in 1979 by
THE HARVESTER PRESS LIMITED
*Publisher: John Spiers*
2 Stanford Terrace, Hassocks, Sussex

and in the USA by
HUMANITIES PRESS INC.,
Atlantic Highlands, N.J. 07716

© This translation, 1979, The Harvester Press Ltd.

*British Library Cataloguing in Publication Data*

Brandell, Gunnar
 Freud - a Man of His Century
 1. Freud, Sigmund 2. Psychoanalysts - Biography
 1. Title
 150'.19'52      BF173.F85

 ISBN 0-85527-515-4

*Humanities Press Inc.*
ISBN 0-391-00871-4

Typeset by Inforum Ltd., Portsmouth
Printed and bound in Great Britain by
Redwood Burn Ltd., Trowbridge and Esher

# Contents

## Translator's Note

The history of this short but close-textured study is well worth recording here. In its earliest form it appeared in Swedish as an essay entitled 'Freud och sekulslutet' (Freud and the turn of the century) in Professor Brandell's collection *Vid seklets källor* [To this century's sources] (Stockholm, 1961). It was subsequently published in Danish (1963) and French (1967). Separate publication in Swedish followed in 1970 under the title *Freud och hans tid* (Freud and his time). The author's latest reformulations and additions were incorporated in the German translation *Freud - Kind seiner Zeit*, published in Munich in 1976, and I have followed this version in preparing my own final text which Professor Brandell has kindly checked and approved.

I am also grateful to my wife (whose first language it is) for disentangling me from more than one syntactical knot in the German and to the London Library and Cambridge University Library who were an unfailing source of books.

Where these have existed I have made use of available English translations of works quoted in the text - for example, the *Standard Edition* of the works of Freud. Elsewhere, for example in the cases of Kleinpaul, Brandes's *Menschen und Werke*, the Schnitzler play and the Strindberg story I have been obliged to make my own versions. The notes have, of course, been reworked to take into account my use of available English sources and, in some instances, I have inserted explanatory notes of my own or added briefly to the existing notes.

Cambridge, May 1978                    Iain White

## Author's Foreword

Today even the opponents of psychoanalysis no longer deny that 'Freudian thought' has after all acquired a far-reaching significance for psychiatry and psychology and, in the most general sense, for the conception of man in the twentieth century. The effects Freud's teachings have had on literature and art, and on cultural and social discussion as a whole are boundless. It was therefore a decisive incident in cultural history when, in the final years of the nineteenth century, the young Sigmund Freud carried out the self-analysis which became the basis for his *Traumdeutung* (Leipzig and Vienna, 1900). With it began the 'psychoanalytic movement' which embraces not only the narrow circle about Freud and his faithful disciples but also such renegades as Alfred Adler, Carl Gustav Jung, Poul Bjerre and (to the extent to which Freudianism became for them a stumbling-block) also some of his adversaries. In addition there is that long line of psychologists, writers and philosophers, stretching from Eugen Bleuler to - I venture to suggest - Jean-Paul Sartre who, without in any strict sense being psychoanalysts, were crucially influenced by Freud. Taken as a whole they add up to a formidable group.

For that reason, as thinker, man and physician, Freud is a part of the general intellectual and cultural history, a history that cannot be followed out in a selective manner but rather must allow of heterogeneous, mutually supplementary viewpoints. Thus it comes about that the breakthrough of Freudian thinking has already been illuminated from various angles and studied in a whole series of useful works of research, to which I here make only the briefest reference. If we leave to one side Ernest Jones's *Sigmund Freud: life and work* (London, 1953-7), the foundation of all general Freud studies, the critical advance in Freud's thought was first studied in the Frenchman Didier Anzieu's *L'Auto-analyse de Freud* (Paris, 1959). It was through him that the notion of Freud's self-analysis first took on a concrete and specific significance. The Swede Ola Andersson wrote (against a background of contemporary clinical discussions) in his *Studies in the Prehistory of Psychoanalysis* (Stockholm, 1962) a fundamental work on the early development of Freud's ideas, while the Swiss-American Henri F. Ellenberger, in *The Discovery of the Unconscious* (London, 1970) presents a view of the psychoanalytical movement as a whole in the light of western intellectual history.

The task I have set myself in the present study is essentially more limited. For some time before its first appearance in 1961, on account in particular of my preoccupation with August Strindberg, I had been fascinated by the interrelation between Freud's thinking and certain currents in the literature of his time. What was in question, then, was the novel and the drama in the nineteenth century - for if the effects of Freud's work belong wholly to the twentieth century, the period of his intellectual formation falls within the final decade of the expiring nineteenth century, and especially that current commonly called 'psychological naturalism', that is to say the movement which in France, Scandinavia and the German-speaking countries can be said to have originated with the Goncourt brothers and Hippolyte Taine, continued with writers such as Ibsen and towards the end of the century, with Paul Bourget, merged almost imperceptibly into symbolism.

In this context the question of the young Freud's reading becomes one of great importance. With the publication of Jones's biography we have learned that Freud took a lively interest in literature and the theatre: with such favourite concepts as 'catharsis' and the 'Oedipus complex' he was, so to speak, already reaching out from the clinical realm into that of literature. Freud was enormously well-read in imaginative literature of the most varied sorts, and hence one may systematically study his reading as part of Freud's biography - as Peter Bruckner has recently done in his *Sigmund Freuds Privatlektüre* (Cologne, 1975).

For me however the question has been to discover points of contact between Freud and the broadly 'depth-psychology-oriented' literature of the turn of the century. This task was not made any the easier by the fact that Freud's extensive correspondence - the publication of a useful accumulation from the last years of the century notwithstanding - is still not available in its entirety. Nevertheless, quite apart from the more general parallels, I believe I have found in the literature I have examined sufficient concrete points of contact to conclude that 'psychological naturalism', and in particular that of France and Scandinavia, was an important factor in the formation of Freudian thinking. In this book the reader can scrutinize the material and judge for himself whether, in my thesis, I have overshot the mark or in fact I have been unduly cautious.

Autumn 1975                                    Gunnar Brandell

*So one still remains a child of one's age, even with something one thinks is one's very own.*

Freud in 1897

# 1  Freud and literature

TOWARDS the middle of March 1900 Georg Brandes visited Vienna, and there he gave a lecture. Among his audience was Doctor Sigmund Freud, then aged forty-three, and still unknown beyond a narrow circle of colleagues and patients. As he relates in a letter to his friend Fliess, he was not much interested in the theme of Brandes's address, and the lecturer's German was harsh and ill-pronounced. Nevertheless he found the Danish critic's words 'refreshing'. Listening, Freud 'revelled' in what the lecturer had to say and, next day, at the prompting of his wife, Martha, he sent Brandes in his hotel a copy of his recently published *The Interpretation of Dreams*.[1]

Freud rarely showed such enthusiasm. Whilst he was unrestrained in his admiration for a piece of scientific work or for a work of creative literature, he was generally very reserved as regards individuals. The refreshment he drew from listening to Brandes's lecture recalls the sentiments he felt when, ten years earlier, he was being taught by Charcot at the Salpêtrière. In each case Freud called to witness a European authority to find support in face of the cramped and parochial public opinion that dominated in Vienna, where his protracted labours had not yet met with approbation. Brandes, moreover, represented Europe's emancipated Jewry. Himself a Jew, Brandes had, in the name of the ideas of the Enlightenment, overcome religious resistance and racial prejudice and now associated on equal terms with ministers and duchesses while, from day to day, Freud had to experience the separation of the races in a Vienna where antisemitism poisoned the atmosphere.

1

But the episode also had a bearing upon the history of ideas. To make one's appeal to Brandes in 1900 was to refer oneself at the same time to the liberal radicalism that had make its breakthrough at the end of the nineteenth century. In the German-speaking world of the time, Brandes stood forth as the protector of modernism and opposition. He was known as the spokesman of French naturalism and Scandinavian social criticism. He had renewed interest in the *Jungen Deutschland* of Heine and Börne, and he had recently assured the fame of Nietzsche, hitherto practically unknown in his own country. In sending Brandes *The Interpretation of Dreams* Freud was declaring his solidarity with this radical orientation; equally, perhaps, he was making it plain that he would not object to being included among Brandes' discoveries and rediscoveries.

Around 1900 Freud was attempting to direct his conceptions - and his ambitions - towards a wider domain than that of medicine. In his first works, as his biographer Ernest Jones describes in considerable detail, his orientation was strictly neurological. However, French influences and his interest in hypnotism, suggestion and the phenomena of hysteria had, at the beginning of the 1890s, increasingly led him to a psychological viewpoint - one little favoured by medical men and natural scientists. In fact this method, which tended to draw conclusions from the analysis of individual lives or of introspection, led him to the literary interpretation of personalities. Already in his first book, *Studies on Hysteria*, published in 1895 in collaboration with Josef Breuer, Freud had stated, albeit with a modicum of regret, that the accounts given by patients were comparable to 'short stories' and 'as one might say, they lack the serious stamp of science'.[2]

Scarcely a year later he no longer had need to express regrets when, in a letter to his friend Fliess in 1896, he spoke of his evolution: 'When I was young, the only think I longed for was Philosophical knowledge, and now that I am going over from medicine to psychology I am in the process of attaining it.'[3] As he had foreseen, he was to take the decisive step in writing *The Interpretation of Dreams*.

In so doing Freud was also to leave behind him the methods of the natural sciences. If we define the scientific method - very schematically - as the art of drawing conclusions on the basis of experimental fact susceptible of being controlled by others, we can see that one could scarcely depart further than Freud had done in his *Interpretation of Dreams*. The scientific elements embodied in the book are only accessories. Freud's interpretation of the nature of dreams rests in the first place on the introspection of his own dreams, his 'auto-analysis', that is to say on matters wholly recalcitrant to control and, from the scientific point of view, as 'lacking in probative value' as J.-J. Rousseau's description of his daydreams in *Les Rêveries d'un promeneur solitaire*. On the other hand he gives freer rein to his literary dispositions than he had as yet done. A considerable body of literary citations illustrates the exposition, bearing witness to a breadth of reading far greater than was common, even in cultured circles. The description and interpretation of the dream-material is uninterruptedly developed by means of short narratives interspersed through the text and strung on a thread of code-breaking, similar to that which holds the reader's attention in certain of Edgar Allan Poe's tales. Read in another order than that - dictated by the exigencies of theoretical demonstration - in which it now stands, *The Interpretation of Dreams* contains, as Anzieu has pointed out, a complete auto-biography of Freud; one might add that there are also to be found therein many elements bearing upon the history of morals in Imperial Vienna.

This method, perfected in *The Interpretation of Dreams*, a method which links the formation of theories in the natural sciences with the literary description of human lives, has made its mark on the entire psycho-analytic movement that had its beginnings shortly after the publication of the book. It conditions more-over the position of psychoanalysis in modern thought. Freud's manner of thinking met with as little approbation in academic quarters as it has achieved of overwhelming success in literature, and in general in the world of ideas in the new century, both as therapeutic doctrine and intellectual ferment. Already the publication of *Studies on Hysteria* had brought a presage of what was to come. While specialists in the subject preserved a guarded silence, Freiherr Alfred von Berger, professor of Literary History, dramatist and, later, director of the Burgtheater in Vienna, wrote a review for the *Neue Freie Presse* - 'a very sensitive article', Freud was to remark in a letter.[4] What is more, von Berger was to take Breuer's and Freud's hints on the catharsis treatment as his point of departure when, two years later, he investigated the content of Aristotle's doctrine of catharsis. No doubt Freud was hoping for a similar result when he sent Brandes a copy of *The Interpretation*.[5]

The source materials and recently published biographical studies have given a clearer picture than that hitherto available of the development of psychoanalysis. 'Freudian thought' was formed in its broad outlines with *The Interpretation of Dreams*, around the turn of the century. Many of the Freudian theories concerning the libido, infantile sexuality, the death instinct and transference are, to be sure, simply not to be found; the Oedipus complex is present only as a preliminary sketch. However most of these later developments in psychoanalytical theory never won wide acceptance; furthermore many points remain obscure regarding the role of the disciples in the psychoanalytic 'movement' in the future evolution of these theories. If by Freud's manner of thinking we understand everything that, as a natural element, went to make up the creation of literary characters and the fashioning, the configuration of discursive human thought, then we find it all in Freud, the solitary of the 1890s: the confrontation in the inner life between the unconscious and the conscious, the psychogenetic viewpoint, the symbolic interpretation of symptoms and dreams, the concern with the dominant role of the sexual and the idea of the therapeutic importance of the conscious.

Many have spoken of the importance of this new 'deep psychological aspect' for the literary description of characters in the 1900s, and indeed for the new poetical language. The name of Freud is cited with complete naturalness in discussion, whether it be of O'Neill, Joyce, Thomas Mann or the surrealists.[6] The other, related aspect of the question is less often raised, namely whether the interior, psychological viewpoint was, in its turn, a product of the climate of ideas that prevailed at the end of the nineteenth century. Freud's official biographer, Ernest Jones, scrupulously chronicles what the young Freud learned from the medical teachers of Vienna and what he rejected of their teaching, but he does not seek to discover whether Freud's presentation of the human personality has certain traits in common with the psychology of Taine or Bourget, Zola or Ibsen. On this point

Freud's own attitude has become the rule in most expositions. He willingly referred to literary authorities, from Sophocles to Maupassant, but always to prove the soundness of his opinions and not with the view to clarifying his own point of departure. Thus the perspective for the history of ideas becomes blurred. The problem of knowing just why the climate of ideas in the 1890s and 1900s conduced to discoveries such as Freud's is slurred over. A summary account will be given here, but it is necessary at the outset to underline that it has no connection with the 'truth' of Freud's theses nor with their 'value', but concerns the dependence on temporal situations, a dependence he shares with others, even the greatest of creators. 'So one still remains a child of one's age, even with something one had thought was one's very own',[7] Freud wrote to Fliess in 1897, at a period when his new ideas were in full effervescence.

It is necessary in this context to present another point of view. Psychoanalytic thought was not of Freud's sole creation. Even during the long period when he had neither encouraging colleagues nor pupils about him. Freud could count on his patients as collaborators. When Freud abandoned hypnotic treatment to employ in its place a therapy of conversation, every treatment took on the aspect of teamwork aimed at the tracking-down of the psyche's secrets. Freud guided the patient but, at the same time, he let the patient guide him. Under these conditions it is impossible, in fact, to judge who is responsible for one or other of the psychological interpretations. It is evident that the field left open to external influences was enlarged in proportion to the number of persons thus putting primary materials at Freud's disposal; Freud shows himself conscious of this state of affairs when, in speaking of various cases, he cites as a reason for discretion the fact that his patients belong to 'an educated and literate social class'.[8] Even if Freud had personally wished to be a scholar, voluntarily isolated in his study, interested only in his researches, his own method of work would have led him into wider domains.

However the young Freud was anything but isolated or detached from cultural events in general. In his chapter on Freud's betrothal period Jones assures us he was a 'great reader' and goes on to enumerate a long list of literary works he hoped his fiancée would read, ranging from the *Odyssey* to Brandes's *Moderne Geister*. Referring to a later period, that which gave rise to *The Interpretation of Dreams*, Jones affirms still more emphatically that: 'In those years Freud read enormously, as his library testified',[9] confirming this with a new list of the poets, novelists, historians, art-historians and archaeologists Freud was studying. He travelled to the extent that his work and his financial position permitted, going for preference to places where he still found traces of ancient culture. He frequently visited the theatre. Finally, if we are to judge from the many allusions to this subject in his letters and in his books, the current political situation was not unknown to him. With friends such as the hellenist Gompertz and the physician Fliess he could exchange ideas on all conceivable subjects, even those far removed from psychopathology. All-in-all Freud must have been, more than the greater part of his colleagues, perfectly aware of what was going on in his epoch - those final years of the nineteenth century that were for him so decisive.

## II  Psychological naturalism

IF Freud the physician was drawing close to literature, literature for its part had for long and in large measure been drawing closer to medicine. The new system of Freud concerning psychological understanding and his self-analysis of the 1890s were, from a certain standpoint, the very apogee of a long collaboration between humanistic men of letters on the one hand and enquiring medical men on the other. The only difference between them is that hitherto the former group had been almost wholly the receivers: with Freud the benefit became more reciprocal.

For many successive generations of realist and naturalist novelists such as Balzac and Flaubert, Zola and Maupassant, it had - as Hans Lindström has shown in his *Hjärnornas kamp* - been of capital importance to keep *au fait* with the latest experiments of medical science. They would constantly refer themselves to clinical observation to provide a basis for the literary interpretation of characters, just as they often took the novel itself as a form of scientific study. This medico-literary collaboration in the Paris of the 1880s reached its culminating point during the period when Jean-Martin Charcot was professor of neurology at the Salpêtrière.

While Freud was following Charcot's course during the winter of 1885-6 he was on occasion invited into the professor's home and came into contact with a highly literary *milieu* - which contrasted with the strictly academic relationships he had known in Vienna. Charcot was something of an oracle for men of letters and associated more often with writers such as Daudet and Turgenev than with his medical colleagues. His lectures and demonstrations were attended not only by physicians from many countries but were also elegant social events where one might encounter as well known a writer as Maupassant or a traveller from afar - Björnson, for example. Naturally medical and literary interests could at times clash. It is reported that at the first night of the stage version of the Goncourts' psychological study *Germinie Lacerteux*, in 1888, Charcot hissed his disapproval from his box. Noting the incident in his *Journal*,[1] Edmond de Goncourt writes a few lines revealing the rivalry between medical men and writers: 'So he disapproves, then, of my having concerned myself since I first began writing with nervous illnesses? Is it that he would like to have a monopoly of the subject?' It was, as we shall see, an opposition that went deeper than the merely personal.

During his sojourn in Paris and in the years that immediately followed, Freud's admiration for Charcot was boundless. The great neurologist, in whom de Goncourt had discovered 'the physiognomy at once of a charlatan and a visionary',[2] was for Freud the agency of intellectual experiences that made a clean sweep of his image of the universe.

Charcot [he wrote to his fiancée, Martha Bernays, on 24 November 1885], who is one of the greatest physicians and a man whose common sense borders on genius, is simply wrecking all my aims and opinions. I sometimes come out of his lectures as from out of Notre Dame, with an entirely new idea about perfection. But he exhausts me; when I come away from him I no longer have any desire to work at my own silly things; it is three whole days since I have done any work, and I have no feelings of guilt. My brain is sated as after an even-

ing in the theatre. Whether the seed will ever bear
fruit, I don't know; but what I do know is that no
other human being has ever affected me in the
same way.[3]

When Charcot died a few years later, Freud wrote
his obituary for the *Wiener medizinische Wochen-
schrift* - a marvellous example of his faculty of charac-
terizing persons, in which he was at once loyal and
objective in his appreciation. In this article Charcot's
work was shown in a historical light.[4] Freud held that
Charcot had given to the study of nervous illness, and
in particular that of hysteria, its 'dignity'; he declared
also that Charcot had established a system of neuro-
pathological maladies allowing the classification of a
great number of elements and recognizing, despite
then-current opinion, the existence of hysteria among
men as well as women. But Charcot, Freud went on to
state, confined himself to pure description; 'he took
only the road an observer completely without precon-
ceived ideas would have chosen', and Freud develops
his idea in a passage that assumes the character of a
landmark:

> . . . if I find someone in a state which bears all the
> signs of a painful affect - weeping, screaming, and
> raging - the conclusion seems probable that a
> mental process is going on in him of which those
> physical phenomena are the appropriate expres-
> sion. A healthy person, if he were asked, would be
> in a position to say what impression it was that
> was tormenting him; but the hysteric would
> answer that he did not know. The problem would
> at once arise of how it is that a hysterical patient is
> overcome by an affect about whose cause he

asserts that he knows nothing. If we keep to our conclusion that a corresponding psychical process *must* be present, and if nevertheless we believe the patient when he denies it; if we bring together the many indications that the patient is behaving as though he *does* know about it; and if we enter into the history of the patient's life and find some occasion, some trauma, which would appropriately evoke precisely those expressions of feeling - then everything points to one solution: the patient is in a special state of mind in which all his impressions or his recollections of them are no longer held together by an associative chain, a state of mind in which it is possible for a recollection to express its affect by means of somatic phenomena without the group of other mental processes, the ego, knowing about it or being able to intervene to prevent it. If we had called to mind the familiar psychological difference between sleep and waking, the strangeness of our hypothesis might have seemed less.[5]

A little earlier in the same year, in collaboration with Breuer, Freud had already articulated the fundamental notion of 'repression' in the 'Vorläufige Mitteilung', the 'Preliminary Communication' that later became the Introduction to *Studies on Hysteria*. In the Charcot obituary Freud refers to the researches being carried on at the same time by Pierre Janet. This conception implies in principle that the domain explicable in psychological terms extends well beyond that which Charcot considered possible or even admissible, supposing, side by side with interior reasons of which the ego is conscious, other reasons, unknown to the ego, which orient the behaviour of the hysterical individual. Thus the old idea that the hysteric 'simulates' - an idea which Charcot had dispelled - returns after a certain fashion, but under a new guise; the patient does not in any sense 'feign' illness, but one portion of the individual is placed, like a screen before the other.

It is more than probable that Freud was led by his wide literary reading to seek a solution to the problem in psychological terms. Few writers, although trusting in Charcot's scientific authority, were in fact disposed to be satisfied with no more than a clinical description providing only external details, when it was their intention to make experimental medicine of use to literature. The very nature of the novel impelled them to supplement medical observation with psychological illustration, improvised perhaps, but more detailed. From a general standpoint this is true even of Zola who, among the naturalists, was the one most oriented towards external description. This is even more evidently true of the Goncourt brothers who, in the older generation, were the precursors of the *fin du siècle*, psychologically-oriented naturalist novel.

Well before Charcot had begun to interest himself in that malady the Goncourts had furnished the classical literary description of a hysterical crisis. *Germinie Lacerteux* (1864) was based on the writers' personal recollections of a faithful and dearly-loved domestic who, after her death, turned out to have been alcoholic and nymphomaniac; she had likewise fleeced her employers without their being aware of it. The writers, it would seem, had with their own eyes seen the hysterical attack described in the book - the tremblings and bodily convulsions, the troubled breathing and the symptoms of pain appear to be observed with all imaginable exactitude. But this could as easily have been lifted from a medical textbook. It is more important in this connection that the Goncourts apparently consider the attack and the other symptoms of Germinie's illness as a cardinal point in her destiny and in the evolution of her personality. The immediate cause that unleashed the crisis was the news of her child's death, and when, later on, other nervous troubles of the same order come about, they are provoked by the hardships linked to the double life Germinie is leading. The viewpoint is throughout psychological, and the antecedents have been traced back to the moment when, still a young girl, Germinie was raped by an old manservant; long afterwards, it is said, she could not bear to have a man come near her but 'involuntarily drew back, trembling and nervous, as if stricken with the same fear as a distraught animal striving to escape'.[6] Freud would most likely have been inclined to attach more importance than the Goncourt brothers to that first 'trauma', and he would perhaps have probed still further back in time as he did in 'Katherina' (a narrative which he presents a clinical journal included in the *Studies on Hysteria*), but he would have approved the direction the interpretation takes. He would furthermore have recognized the situation of many of his consultations, with or without hypnosis in the scene in which the Goncourts have Germinie talk in her sleep in 'a voice heavy with the mystery and shuddering of the night, in which the sleeper seemed to be searching gropingly for memories and passing her hand over faces'.[7] When she spoke of a death she would, in Freud's view, have been expressing the wish to see her faithless lover dead; he would similarly have interpreted - and appreciated - the scene in which Germinie reads the future in the coffee-grounds and sees a cross next to the image of her favoured rival.

The information at present at our disposal does not

allow us to judge whether or not Freud knew the Goncourt brothers' novel, but *Germinie Lacerteux* was one of the points of departure of the rich literature of psychopathological characters that sprang up around 1890, and Freud could have met with similar ideas in many quarters. It is characteristic of the writers that, unlike the majority of medical men, they should be capable of identifying to a greater or less extent with the sick persons they depict, and thus provide an understanding account of the maladies. Paul Hervieu developed this device so far in his controversial novel *L'Inconnu*, published in 1887, that by the final chapter the reader is not sure which among the characters are sane and which are insane.

Of particular interest in this connection was Strindberg's study of hysteria in his long story 'Genvägar' ('Secret Paths'). It had been presented to the Swedish public under the title 'En Häxa' ('A Witch') in the guise of a historical narrative in the collection *Svenska öden* (Swedish Destinies), but was published in the original version in the Vienna *Neue Freie Presse* in August and September 1887. Freud was at that time in Austria and his interest in hysteria had already been aroused by Charcot; it is therefore probable that he paid some attention to the story.

Strindberg's 'Genvägar' was an entirely typical expression of his then current scientific-naturalist ambitions. His point of departure was an encounter with a woman who claimed to be a spirit medium. Strindberg considered she had a hysterical tendency and on this basis sought in her previous life for reasons that might have brought her to this pass. In so doing he availed himself of the psychological literature that was to hand. The fundamental notion of his interpretation - that the woman in question (Tekla in the story) cultivated her unhealthy states to advance her social position - was borrowed, according to Hans Lindström, from the French psychiatrist Charles Richet.[8] This idea was expressed more crudely in the second part of the story, where Strindberg's anti-feminism comes to the surface and the writing becomes banal. But initially he gives an intense description, founded on personal experience, of the formation of a hysterical character. In an even more evident way than the Goncourts he relates it to a traumatic experience in early youth. A few days before her confirmation the pastor had invited the young members of the sodality to a meeting, and there Tekla had been kissed by a handsome youth. This had thrown her into an ecstatic state in which religious feelings, newly awakened sexuality and distress were strangely blended.

> Then she heard the voice of the Lord: *Peace be with you*; the arms slackened their embrace, she faltered and fell back as if in a dream and saw the red flame of the lamp standing over the dark and beautiful features, like the Holy Spirit over the heads of the disciples at Emmaus; she saw the black and stern faces on the wall looking on with sidelong eyes; then the limping beadle came and closed the stove-door. She halted at the cemetery gate and relived the vision from the beginning; she opened her coat and breathed in the scent of lily of the valley that rose from the bosom of her dress and bent her head to kiss the brown bombazine; but the collar was too tight about her throat. And, look! A white plant was growing up and to the right, with six sleek little bell-like flowerheads on a clear-yellow stem between two dark green leaves, and it was climbing up between her young

breasts towards her mouth to be kissed. A shudder passed through her breasts, as if the milk were seeking to spurt from them and her legs were trembling so much she had to support herself against the heavy, wrought-iron gates. At that moment she heard a bugle call from the town square, a bell was ringing without cease, dogs were barking, boys were shouting and a sound echoed the length of the narrow street, a thin yet muffled crashing sound as of hammered brass; it grew stronger, swelled, came closer, enormous, red as the fiery glow that lit up the signs and the tombs and the little square windowpanes; it drew closer and now there came four black horses with fiery eyes and fiery harness, and a blood-red waggon with golden-helmeted men, running in sweat, passed swiftly by, and on the waggon were black serpents curled about blood-red casks with brass taps, and all the while the bell rang and the light of the fire was shining on the waggon.[9]

It is, of course, the fire brigade responding to an urgent call, but at the same time it stands as a symbol of the distress evoked by sexuality, just as the vision of the flower growing out of her side is a symbol of Tekla's sexual hopes.

Freud's patients were of course also to witness in symbolic fashion to their unconscious impulses. If Freud, the future revealer of unconscious death wishes had come upon Strindberg's story, he would without any doubt have read attentively the passage in which Tekla, seated at her mother's deathbed, catches herself wishing she were already dead and immediately attempts to 'repress' the thought.

One could multiply these instances of parallels

between Freud's researches and those one encounters in the literature of the time, drawing in particular on the writings of Bourget, Maupassant and Ola Hansson. Naturally this does not mean that Freud would have arrived at his conclusions by means of novel-reading. It means only that, in respect of the direction his researchers were taking, he was at one with the psychology of the modern novel. Besides, when one is dealing with parallels of the sort cited above, there is no need to provide literary documents, as for example with Sophocles or Shakespeare, with an interpretation, more or less forced as the case may be, in order to declare that they are in line with the findings of Freud. Writers such as the Goncourts and Strindberg had, on the whole, access to much the same ideo-historical data as had Freud: they knew a great deal about hysteria and a great deal about the unconscious and there can be little doubt that on the plane of ideas they were seeking for something of much the same order as he was seeking. These writers were to some extent men of science, and the man of science was to a tolerable degree also a man of letters: they had a point in common: both grounded themselves on the naturalist doctrine.

## III   *Positivism and pessimism*

THE fundamental ideas of naturalism consisted above all in a belief in science, in the conviction that the epoch of religion was at an end and that it would give place in the future to scientific reason. In writing *The Future of an Illusion* Freud was reviving an opinion widespread in his youth but at that time, 1927, no longer so much current. Freud summed up his position in a letter written in January 1927; in it he shows himself to be a loyal disciple of Comte: 'In secret - one cannot say such things aloud - I believe that one day metaphysics will be condemned as a nuisance, as an abuse of thinking, as a survival from the period of the religious *Weltanschauung*.'[1] The orthodoxy of the positivism is underlined in its formulation; it is not merely Christianity, not even merely religion but metaphysics in general that Freud rejects.

But in the background was something quite other than the optimism of Comte. The ageing Freud knew better than most of his contemporaries just how irrational were men's impulses; his trust in reason was a belief he held to, not in consequence of, but despite what he knew. He called for the furtherance of the truth, although he knew well that men cling stubbornly to their illusions and sometimes, as Freud also admitted, had need of them.

We search in vain in French naturalist literature for the problems that left their mark on *The Future of an Illusion*. Not once did those authors who later went back on their positivist convictions - Huysmans is a typical example - ask themselves whether they might have need of an illusion in order to live. On the other hand the question of illusions, of the cogency for

18

human existence of the 'life-giving lie', was an important theme in the 'advanced' literature of the Scandinavian countries. There the propaganda for the new scientific thinking was accompanied by a persistent and anxious questioning: *How much truth can a man bear?* The prevailing tone of the 'advanced' Scandinavian literature is marked with hesitation before the new perspectives that were being opened up. Strindberg, Ibsen and J.P. Jacobsen all posed the question of how the new man, freed from his illusions and from religion, would in fact manage to live.

Freud had already confronted these problems before he formulated his psychoanalytic method, and the experience had made a deep impression upon him. In October 1895 he read Jens Peter Jacobsen's *Niels Lyhne*. He wrote to Fliess: 'The Jacobsen (N.L.) has moved me more than anything I have read in the last nine years. The last chapters seem to me classic.'[2] This testifies to a high estimation: nine years previously Freud had been translating Charcot's work into German and thus preparing for his passage from neurology to psychology.

In the discussions that are carried on in Jacobsen's novel it is first and foremost Niels Lyhne who is the spokesman for optimistic atheism. His interlocutor, Hjerrild, also adheres to the atheistic standpoint but he is not convinced that 'a new heaven and a new earth' will arise after the collapse of Christianity.[3] Employing sarcastic turns of phrase that directly call to mind the title of Freud's book of 1927, he gives vent to his pessimistic atheism: 'After all, atheism is unspeakably tame. Its end and aim is nothing but a disillusioned humanity. The belief in a God who rules everything and judges everything is humanity's last great illusion, and when that is gone, what then? Then you are wiser;

but richer, happier? I can't see it.'[4]

In the two final chapters which Freud thought of as 'classical', the problems of atheism take on a new acuteness in the contrast between two different ways of dying. Gerda Lyhne had been converted by Niels to atheism, but in her last extremity she dare not die without the support of religion and in the end becomes once more 'the little girl who went to church clinging to her mother's hand and sat there shivering with cold and wondering why people sinned so much'.[5] Niels himself refuses to follow this road, although Doctor Hjerrild brushes aside his scruples of conscience. Rather than call up 'bright, tender memories from our childhood'[6] and let himself be consoled by illusions, he dreams in his delirium that he must 'die standing'.[7] Despite the defeat of his life he still has spirit enough for a final act of defiance.

This character has moral stature; but there is no trace of the positivist confidence of which Lyhne previously spoke with such eloquence. In Jacobsen's disillusioned eyes man appears from the start ready to abandon the struggle and enter, like Madame Boye, into a state of bourgeois quietude or, like Gerda Lyhne, to become a child again; his situation is precarious, his self-esteem is constantly threatened and he cannot, without the greatest effort, see life as it really is. A comparable stoicism may be found in Freud's work on religion and, in general in his conception of the difficulties of human life, formed as it was in the course of his therapeutic experience. When he became acquainted with Niels Lyhne's sombre faith in the credo of the Enlightenment, nourished as it was by his pietistic heritage, Freud recognized in it something that accorded with the image that he was himself in the process of forming.

Chance, but not chance alone, brought it about that, five years after having read Jacobsen's book, Freud was to hear Brandes speak on a theme comparable to that of the last chapters of *Niels Lyhne*. Brandes's lecture was concerned with books and reading, but he concluded it with an appeal to his audience that they should fight to the finish for their convictions; and he illustrated this idea with the story of General Moureau who consented to the surrender of Soissons, just before the Emperor Napoleon sent relief. He had had seven hundred men against fifty thousand; but, said Brandes, he would nonetheless have been impelled to hold out: unconditional fidelity to a vocation, to a truth, is the point in the universe where a solution is found. This is the same soldierly fidelity that Niels Lyhne displayed in his struggle against the powers of heaven. Freud's comments reveal the extent to which the lecture pleased him: 'Such a severe conception of life is unknown to us; our petty logic, and our petty conventionality, are different from their northern equivalents.'[8] Brandes in his lecture - or confession of faith - acknowledged Kierkegaard as the source of the moral attitudes of advanced Scandinavian thinkers. From that source there springs a current of ideas which runs down to Freud and which contributed to forming the attitudes of a man who, for a long period of his life, deserved more than any other to be called 'the solitary'.

These radical views, which Freud shared with the naturalists in general and with the advanced Scandinavian writers in particular, were expressed by him in the epigraph he chose for *The Interpretation of Dreams*: '*Flectere si nequeo superos, Acheronta movebo*' ('If I cannot bend the higher powers, I will move the infernal regions'). Freud had not drawn his motto directly from the *Aeneid*: in January 1927 he wrote in a letter to Werner Achelis that he had borrowed it from Ferdinand Lassalle 'in whose case it was probably meant personally and relating to social - not psychological - classifications'.[9] Erich Fromm remarks, with just cause, that the borderline between Freud's social and psychological views was not always as clear as he thought, and that what we have here is an unconscious identification on Freud's part with the great socialist leader and unflinching rebel.

This is a conclusion that springs immediately to mind. Yet it is by no means certain that, as Fromm supposes, Freud was directly inspired by Lassalle when he set that epigraph at the head of *The Interpretation of Dreams*. Here too it is possible that the advanced literature of the Scandinavians may have been an intermediary source. The verse from the *Aeneid* appears on the title page of a pamphlet Lassalle published in 1859, *Der italienische Krieg und die Aufgabe Preussens* (The Italian War and Prussia's Mission). It immediately occurs to one to conclude that this was the book Freud took with him when, in July 1899, he travelled to Berchtesgaden with the completed manuscript of *The Interpretation of Dreams*: 'In addition to my manuscript I am taking the "Lassalle" and a few works on the unconscious to Berchtesgaden.'[10] This is what Fromm too supposes. But on closer investigation it seems improbable that Freud would have found it worth the trouble, forty years after the event, to study a pamphlet written in a very specific situation for immediately contemporary purposes. Lassalle's work expresses nothing in the way of an explicitly social tendency, but it expresses to perfection the nationalist side of his thinking. When, in 1859, Napoleon III sanctioned his troops' penetration into Italy, Lassalle demanded of the Prussian government that it seize the opportunity and strike a blow for German unity. Rather than support the Austrians, actively or passively, against Louis Napoleon, the Prussian government should act on the example of France and incorporate Schleswig-Holstein into the German state. In this context the motto from Virgil signified that 'if I cannot compel the government to listen to me, I can at least mobilize public opinion'.

Virgil's line is given a broader treatment in Brandes's book on Lassalle which appeared in German in the early 1880s. In this book it serves as a *Leitmotiv* and becomes a symbolic representation of the entire situation of Lassalle, the militant democrat, a situation which merges with that of Brandes in Denmark, and is equally the programme of a radicalism that has yet to assume power but which, for all that, is not condemned to ineffectualness.

> Lassalle was entirely excluded from all immediate influence upon the Government, and therefore upon the development of society in the State. He stood upon the further side of the great gulf formed by the obscurantism of the petty nobility and revolutionary Radicalism. But Lassalle was by no means excluded from exercising influence indirectly, if he were able to avoid creating unnecessary enemies for himself by attacking the Monarchy in general, or the reigning dynasty, or the Government, or national sentiment, or religion, or hereditary right, and could raise the so-called fourth class from its political impotence, and rouse it to a struggle properly conducted by lawful means, for the purpose of securing social and political equivalence (not equality) with the other classes. This seemed no impossible purpose.

No wonder, therefore, if Lassalle, pondering like
Achilles in his tent, mentally repeated to himself
for nights and days the burden of Virgil's line:
*Flectere si nequeo superos, Acheronta movebo* [11]

In the 1890s Sigmund Freud had every reason to
identify himself with the great solitary. Many years of
work in many branches of medicine had brought him
only grudging recognition. On the part of specialists,
his researches into hysteria and the neuroses had met
with the chilliest of receptions. His hopes of a better
university post seemed non-existent - among other
reasons because of his Jewish origins - and Vienna's
prudes had already made it abundantly clear to him
what a brouhaha he would cause when eventually he
gave clear expression to his thoughts on the importance of sexuality. It is of course also this sense of soli-
tude, almost of rejection, that explains why he so
vehemently threw in his lot with such colleagues as
Breuer and Fliess, in whom he believed he would find
understanding.

## IV  Isolated in Vienna

IN a larger context, seen against a background of the politico-cultural situation as a whole, Freud was not, to be sure, quite as isolated as he sometimes thought; or, to put it better, there were others too who felt themselves alone and overshadowed by the hierarchy of the Empire, by its conformism and its stiff formalism, others who called on the subterranean powers. We have already noted the comprehension with which Alfred von Berger greeted his first work. Some others, belonging to a more open opposition, call for mention, the more so because Freud was not unaware of the affinities between their efforts and his own.

In January 1906 Freud addressed himself to Karl Kraus - eighteen years his junior - in the following terms: 'That I find my name repeatedly mentioned in the *Fackel* is caused presumably by the fact that your aims and opinions partially coincide with mine.'[1] To be sure the letter was written in a context in which Freud found himself obliged to enlist Kraus's help, but even in such a situation he was not the man to be prodigal with his declarations of solidarity. One asks oneself what similarities Freud could find between himself and the fearsome linguistic inquisitor of *Die Fackel*. That Kraus later developed into a severe critic of psychoanalysis and the 'psychoanals' was moreover, only natural at a period when he considered everything that moved with the times as the expression of a progressive degradation. Nevertheless he wrote about Freud at a time when the latter was still not known and not successful, making use, as Freud notes in his letter, of sympathetic words.

Kraus made his debut at the age of eighteen with an

article in *Die Gesellschaft*, the leading organ of the youthful naturalist literary movement in Vienna. His subject was the difficulties encountered by Max Burckhardt, director of Vienna's richly traditional Burgtheater. Burckhardt had renewed the repertoire and introduced to those venerable boards the works of Ibsen, Hauptmann and other naturalist writers. Who, Kraus demanded, set out to oppose him? He replied to his own question in Ibsen-like terms:

> Not the critics, who have barked but not bitten; no, it was a rigid conservative clique - 'a damnable and dense majority' - set everywhere athwart his path like a brazen wall. Who? properly speaking one cannot say. A spirit opposed to every fresh and new current, so firm and rigid and yet elusive, everywhere brutally unyielding and animal in its stupidity, paralysing and death-dealing: in short the archetype of the Great Boyg in *Peer Gynt*.[2]

Throughout his life as editor of *Die Fackel* Karl Kraus was to give a monumental form to this attitude of the 'solitary' struggling with a rigid public opinion, compared here to the Great Boyg in *Peer Gynt*. It is not surprising that he should have chosen the press as the object of his most bitter contempt if we recall the role 'the hacks' play in Ibsen's dramas, or if we consider Kierkegaard's deeply personal struggle against the boulevard journal *Corsaren*. In the beginning he acted in *Die Fackel* as the intrepid exponent of the truth in a domain that was close to Freud's preoccupations: morality and sexuality. In his book *Sittlichkeit und Kriminalität* (Morality and Criminality), first published in 1908 (the first chapter of which originally appeared in *Die Fackel* in 1902), he violently attacked

the sexual morality of the bourgeoisie and compared it
to prostitution which he found, in spite of all, to be
morally superior. It is beyond doubt of this struggle
that Freud is thinking when he speaks of the affinity
between Kraus's efforts and his own.

It may well be that we are also justified in seeing in
Freud's words an allusion to the fact that he considered himself the inspirer of the younger writers; in
the present instance this supposition is not without
foundation, even if the sexual revolt may have had
numerous other sources in advanced Scandinavian-
German literature. One writer who made use of
Freud's ideas straightforwardly - and openly - was
Kraus's friend Weininger, a still younger representative of the secularized Jewish intelligentsia of Vienna.
Thanks to his book *Geschlecht und Charakter* (1903),
which was widely read and reached its sixth edition
two years after publication, the name of Freud and
something of his theories - those, for example, on the
causes of hysteria and the Oedipus situation - for the
first time reached a broad international public: it
should nonetheless be made plain at this point that
they come together here only as materials in the construction of a system in the manner of Schopenhauer
in which the element 'virility' represents the superior,
spiritual principle, while the element 'femininity' represents base 'materialism' under the rule of sexuality.

Although in the last analysis Weininger comes
closer to an almost gnostic conception of life, he bases
his speculations on physical facts; and he delivers himself over to his theme with a perfect indifference to
what the 'common reader' might consider the decen-
cies. His attitude, like that of Kraus and Freud, is that
of an unconditional seeker after truth, one who lets no
social taboo stand in his way in his search for know-

ledge. In this respect he was a perfect representative of
the naturalist attack on accepted conventions; and the
success his book met with was in great part a *succès de
scandale*.

What was Freud's position concerning Weininger?
In the letter to Kraus mentioned above, he declares he
is unable to share in the great esteem for Weininger
expressed in *Die Fackel* and rather condescendingly
calls him 'the undoubtedly brilliant young man'.[3] Now
as Jones points out, this was a very delicate affair for
Freud. His former friend, Fliess, had launched an
attack on Freud, the dead Weininger and his friend the
philosopher Hermann Swoboda. Freud must,
according to Fliess, have transmitted to his pupil Swoboda an idea, very dear to Fliess, on the 'double'
character of sexuality, namely that each individual
simultaneously possesses masculine and feminine com-
ponents. Swoboda in his turn must - without mention-
ing Fliess - have passed this on to Weininger, who must
then have based his *Geschlecht und Charakter* on the
idea of bisexuality. Was it also true, Fliess added in a
private letter to Freud before their definitive break,
that Freud had known Weininger and read his manuscript?

Jones seems to be of the opinion that the affair
developed much as Fliess had supposed. Freud sought
to make light of the matter when he was implicated,
but indirectly he testified in favour of Fliess regarding
a meeting with Weininger when he wrote to Kraus: '. . .
I myself did not know Weininger before he wrote his
book'.[4] This formulation does not exclude the possibility that he knew him *after* the manuscript of the book
was completed, or indeed that he had read the manuscript.

In this broad connection Ernest Jones challenges

the affirmation of another researcher that 'the famous writers Karl Kraus, Hugo von Hofmannsthal, Arthur Schnitzler and Jakob Wassermann "joined the psychoanalytic circle and made their different contributions to its theories"'.[5] Jones observes that Kraus showed himself, in fact, to be an enemy of psychoanalysis. As we have seen, this did not prevent Freud from considering him to a certain extent a kindred spirit; the same would seem to have been the case with Weininger. And even if, in respect of Freud's literary relationships, it is a gross exaggeration to speak of a 'psychoanalytic circle' or a 'contribution' to the formulation of theories, it would appear that between him and at least one of the above-named writers, namely Arthur Schnitzler, there existed still closer spiritual affinities.

Born in 1862, he was older than the others mentioned, and he had already made his beginnings in literature when Freud first started to publish his psychological theories. As a result of his first successful work, *Anatol* (1893) he was known as the author of half-cynical, half sentimental *proverbes dramatiques* about erotic entanglements. Naturally enough he became involved in conflicts with the guardians of morality: in a letter of 1894, to Georg Brandes, who became his friend, he tells, how his play *Das Märchen*, failed at the Deutsches Volkstheater on account of its 'abandoned morals'.[6] A few years later, as a result of 'a warning from on high', *Freiwild* was withdrawn from the repertoire.[7] Certain of his works - *Leutnant Gustl* (1901) for example - mount a critique, in interior monologue form, of the Vienna of the high bourgeoisie and the aristocracy. In the background, as the enemy of truth and feeling, as the incarnation of bigotry and mendacity, lowers Austrian antisemitism. 'It's amazing what swine we live among here; and I always think it must strike even the antisemites how antisemitism - leaving everything else aside - should, one way or another, have the unique power of bringing to the fore the most mendacious and basest qualities of human nature and raising them to the highest power.'[8] What most pleased Freud about this writer, officially regarded with suspicion and distaste, was precisely that character which had provoked the attack on Schnitzler on the part of the moralists and antisemites: outspokenness regarding erotic matters. Freud expresses this personally and clearly in a letter of congratulation he sent Schnitzler on his fiftieth birthday; in it he states that both he and the recipient of his letter had suffered 'as a consequence of the ridiculous and shameful contempt manifested by men of our time in face of the erotic'.[9]

Consciousness of these 'elective affinities' would not have been so marked in Freud if Schnitzler had been no more than a frivolous and witty controversialist. The erotic contexts in his work were not merely an appropriate occasion for brief and bitter-sweet 'spicy' encounters, as in *Anatol*, but a 'serious matter', closely associated with ethical problems. No one has better characterized this side of Schnitzler's work, or done so as generously, as Freud in a letter written ten years later than the last-mentioned.

> Your determinism as well as your scepticism - what people call pessimism - your preoccupation with the truths of the unconscious and of the instinctive drives in man, your dissection of the cultural conventions of our society, the dwelling of your thoughts on the polarity of love and death; all this moves me with an uncanny feeling of familiarity [...] So I have formed the impres-

sion that you know through intuition - or rather
from detailed self-observation - everything that I
have discovered by laborious work on other
people.[10]

If we wish to appreciate the degree to which Freud
could recognize in Schnitzler 'something one thinks is
one's very own', we have only to study the drama *Paracelsus*. It appeared in 1898; Freud read it in March of
the same year, before *The Interpretation of Dreams*
had been written, and commented as follows: 'I was
astonished to see what such a writer knows about these
things.'[11] We may imagine that at this time he attached
importance to what Schnitzler had to say about
dreams:

> Bedenkt dies Eine nur: dass jede Nacht
> Uns zwingt hinabzusteigen in ein Fremdes,
> Entledigt unsrer Kraft und unsres Richtums,
> Und alles Lebens Fülle und Verdienst
> Von weit geringer Macht sind als die Träume,
> Die unserm willenlosen Schlaf begegnen.[12]

> And remember that each night compels us to
> descend, stripped of our riches and our power,
> into an unknown world; for all life's abundance
> and all its gains weigh lightly against the dreams
> that come to us unbidden in our sleep.

In this dream Paracelsus, with the aid of hypnosis,
shows what lies hidden in the unconscious; he shows
how the faithful wife has, in fact, desired her young
admirer and, in so doing, he teaches her self-
complacent husband, representing the blinkered bourgeoisie, a lesson. Side by side with the daylight self

there is a night self that appears in dreams and secret desires; and we must not feel too sure of ourselves in the clear light of day:

> Ein Sturmwind kam, der hat auf
>     Augenblicke
> Die Tore unsrer Seelen aufgerissen,
> Wir haben einen Blick hineingetan ...
> Es ist vorbei, die Tore fallen zu. -
> Doch was ich heut gesehn, für alle Zeit
> Soll's mich vor allzu grossem Stolze hüten.[13]

A tempest comes which, for a moment, bursts open the doors of our soul; for a moment we look therein ... then it has passed, and once more the doors are shut. But what I have seen today will forever protect me from undue pride.

It is interesting from a chronological viewpoint to note that already, in his first book, Schnitzler was touching upon this same theme. In one of the pieces Anatol hypnotizes his mistress, Cora, in order to discover whether or not she is faithful; but when it comes to the point of posing the decisive question he draws back. Are there not unconscious states of mind, an infidelity perhaps, without responsibility? These determinist and naturalist presuppositions that Schnitzler shared with Freud led logically to a reduction in the significance of the waking and prudential self and a corresponding rehabilitation of the instinctive and unconscious side of man. But at the same time, despite the rationalist point of departure, there is a new opening for the art of atmosphere and for poetic *chiaroscuro*.

If we are called upon to place Schnitzler in the history of literature, it seems most natural to think of

him as a representative of the psychological naturalism that stemmed from Flaubert and the Goncourt
brothers and, by degrees, overtook and surpassed in
success the programme of Zola, directed as it was at
externals. These currents arrived somewhat late in the
German-speaking world, at about the same time as the
advanced Scandinavian writers were meeting with a
favourable reception. A by no means unimportant
movement - part decadent, part naturalist - developed
among the young writers of Berlin, while in Austria on
the other hand, in the strictly hierarchical Empire, the
new ideas seem to have contributed to a still further
alienation of the intellectuals from thier *milieu*. Kraus,
Schnitzler and Weininger - all were examples of the isolation of the 'Jungen Österreich', an isolation that
went hand-in-hand with a spirit of partisanship,
indeed in some instances of fanaticism when the
question arose of asserting the new 'asocial' values. In
the circumstances it seems only natural to consider
Freud as their older *confrère*.

# V  Ibsen and Freud

WHATEVER one may think about the triumph of modernity in Germany and Austria it is plain that, more than any other, Henrik Ibsen was responsible for the intellectual awakening in those countries. His influence reached its highest point in about the 1890s: the theatrical directors of Berlin, Munich and Vienna vied among themselves for a new work from his pen. The key words of his dramas were the common currency of newspaper columns and drawing-room conversation; they could be used and understood without a source being ascribed. With the staging of each new play violent discussions broke out. By 1901 a historian of German literature, Bertold Litzmann, could give his book on Ibsen (it was one among many others) the subtitle *Ein Beitrag zur Geschichte des deutschen Dramas im 19. Jahrhundert* (A Contribution to the History of the German Drama in the Nineteenth Century). In this author's estimation Ibsen, like Shakespeare, had won by his influence a place in German literature. Neither Flaubert nor Zola, Dostoevski or even Strindberg could compete with Ibsen in the German-speaking countries.

Freud was as well acquainted with Ibsen's work as any member of the 'cultured and widely-read' class from which his friends and his patients were drawn. During the first world war he wrote a psychologically based analysis of *Rosmersholm*, but for a long time previously his writings had been rich in allusions to the situations and characters of Ibsen's dramas. When Freud received a copy of a colleague's book (in all probability this was Max Nordau), the following night he dreamed of it, as he recounts in *The Interpretation of*

34

*Dreams*: 'It's written in a positively norekdal style'[1] - a conflation of the names of Nora and Ekdal. The memory of Ibsen penetrated even into his dreams. In the analysis of the '*non vixit*' dream in the same book - a fine demonstration of perspicacity - the notion of a 'ghost' becomes quite specifically the key word.[2] Just as the Chamberlain Osvald returns in ghostly form in the character of his son, so Freud believes he perceives how the new friendly relationships in his life are but a repetition of the *rapport* that existed between himself and his brother in their youth. This same writer did much to add impetus to his thinking on the relation between father and son. After having described the Oedipus complex he declares that 'an author who, like Ibsen, brings the immemorial struggle between fathers and sons into prominence in his writings may be certain of producing his effect'.[3] This may well be an allusion to *Ghosts* or to *The Wild Duck*.

It is entirely plausible that *Ghosts* should in particular have stirred Freud's imagination, and this not merely because Ibsen's chosen theme has its medical or psychological aspects. *Ghosts*, like *Rosemersholm*, belongs to that class among Ibsen's dramas in which the past slowly reveals itself to the audience. Therein lies the true tension of the play. The present action of the play is to all intents and purposes confined to the symbolic burning down of the children's home; the rest is the consequence of an action that took place before the curtain rose. The parallel with Freud's therapeutic analyses is evident. The notes concerning the 'present' of the patient, above all his present conception of his symptoms, are subordinated to the probing of his memories and his past life, carried out under the direction of the analyst. Like Freud's neurotics, the characters of *Ghosts* are under the sway of the past:

But I'm inclined to think that we're all ghosts,
Pastor Manders; it's not only the things that we've
inherited from our fathers and mothers that live
on in us, but all sorts of old dead ideas and old
dead beliefs and things of that sort. They're not
actually alive in us, but they're rooted there all the
same, and we can't rid ourselves of them.[4]

Naturally Madame Alving is not thinking of 'trau-
mas' as Freud seeks to explain them in his patients, but
rather prejudices and the emotional residues of out-
moded convictions. But despite this reservation the
resemblance remains. Halvdan Koht writes that *The
Pillars of the Community, A Doll's House* and *Ghosts*
turn on the same basic problem: 'How is one to escape
the heritage of the past?'[5] This is a question that might
equally be put to Freud's patients as he describes them
in *Studies on Hysteria*, beset with anxiety and dismay
by what lies behind them.

Freud assimilates the views of Ibsen in exactly the
same way as he assimilates the Lassalle/Brandes interpretation of Virgil's line. This latter, as Freud empha-
sizes, is social. The 'powers on high' were those who
ruled over society, the 'infernal regions' were the prole-
tarian masses, standing in expectation of asserting
their rights. When Freud took up the metaphors, he set
both in the individual psyche; with him it is the ego
that rules and the unconscious impulses that seek to
assert themselves. Similarly with *Ghosts*: Madame
Alving, among others, believes that the struggle
between the old and the new 'conceptions' can equally
well be understood as a struggle between men; the
'ghosts' of which Freud speaks live within the individual.

It might appear that undue importance is attached

here to chance literary associations. But it is evident that Freud was aware of the work of the new and radical, at times even revolutionary, writers before he began to develop his psychological theories; and he also sympathized with their views. When certain of their perspectives reappear in his interpretation of the human mind, albeit translated to another 'level', 'interiorized', it is quite natural to consider the radical literature of the time as a creative force in Freud's development and not merely as a source of literary ornamentation. With their struggle in the interests of society's downtrodden, their critique of the morally censorious, their exposure of double standards and of the façades behind which lurked 'the beast in man', the radical writers provided a most opportune model when Freud was working towards a picture of the events taking place in the human psyche.

A parallel of what must have taken place springs insistently to mind. Darwin tells in a letter to Ernst Haeckel of how he was led to think of 'the struggle for life' as a motive force in evolution. He had observed and studied the resemblances between existing and extinct species and had come to the conclusion that they must derive from ancient, common forms.

> But for some years I could not conceive how each form became so excellently adapted to its habits of life. I then began systematically to study domestic productions, and after a time saw clearly that man's selective power was the most important agent. I was prepared, from having studied the habits of animals, to appreciate the struggle for existence, and my work in geology gave me some idea of the lapse of past time. Therefore, when I happened to read 'Malthus on Population', the

idea of natural selection flashed on me.[6]

The reading of Malthus was the determining impetus for the formation of Darwinism. Thus it is difficult to overestimate the importance of Malthus for Darwin, but it would nonetheless be misleading to call him a Malthusian. He was not a disciple; he took from Malthus only that of which he had need, and he transferred the model he had found in Malthus's theory of population to his own domain, where this model served his own purposes. In the same way Freud acquires from Ibsen and other radical writers a *schema* of thought which, transferred to the domain of psychology, seems to him to provide 'the key to the castle'.

That Ibsen should make use in a play of the tension built up by the gradual unravelling of secrets from the past was nothing new, but as a device has belonged since Sophocles' *Oedipus Rex* to the classical formulae of dramatic art. But of course Ibsen gave this procedure a new content in so far as he linked it to the criticism of society. 'Decent society' became for him a brilliant and seemly façade to conceal the memory of crimes and moral defeats. In his radical writings he knew of only one way of dealing with secrets: to admit them openly. The very construction of Ibsen's dramas leads to those great scenes in which the characters 'declare themselves', more or less in the hope that it will be possible, after the ghosts have been laid, to go on living.

The final scene of *The Pillars of the Community* could well be chosen as the typical example of this form of catharsis in Ibsen. The chief character has built his success in life on a lie, dating from his youth, thanks to which he has allowed a faithful friend to take the consequences of his own folly; in addition he has

charged him with a crime he did not commit. Throughout the drama Consul Bernick attempts to protect his
own position but, in the final scene, he openly admits
everything and by this admission he is delivered and a
new, truer life opens up before him: 'Where have I
been? You will be shocked to know. Now I feel as if I
had come to my senses after being poisoned. But what
I do feel is that I can be young and strong again.'[7]

Consul Bernick unburdens his heart in confession.
Breuer and Freud too, in the account of their 'cathartic' method,[8] cite confession as a means of discharging
the 'suppressed affect' in hysteria:[9] 'In other cases
speaking itself is the adequate reflex, when, for
instance, it is a lamentation or giving utterance to a tor-
menting secret, e.g. a confession.'[10] The difference, to
be sure, lies in the fact that with Freud's patients the
troublesome secrets are unconscious while, in Ibsen's
play, Consul Bernick is constantly aware of his act.
But this distinction once made, it is nonetheless striking how closely Ibsen's great scenes of admission and
settlement approach to Freud's psychotherapeutic
method.

The case of Miss Lucy R., detailed in *Studies on
Hysteria*, turns on a governess plagued by an
imaginary odour of burnt milk pudding. Preliminary
investigations established that this odour was associated with a painful situation at Miss Lucy's place of
work. But Freud was not satisfied with this explanation and, one day, he directly laid bare the secret:

> I cannot think that these are all the reasons for
> your feelings about the children. I believe that
> really you are in love with your employer, the
> Director, though perhaps without being aware of
> it yourself, and that you have a secret hope of

taking their mother's place in actual fact. And then we must remember the sensitiveness you now feel towards the servants, after having lived peacefully with them for years. You're afraid of their having some inkling of your hopes and making fun of you.[11]

After this explanation, and after certain other difficulties had been cleared up, the patient became at once more positive and cheerful. When questioned as to whether or not she is still in love with her employer, she replied: 'Yes, I certainly am, but that makes no difference. After all, I can have thoughts and feelings to myself.'[12]

When the secret is laid bare and admitted, when the truth is exposed to the clear light of day, a sense cf release makes its appearance, restoring harmony to the patient. For all its undeniably superficial character, this *dénouement* gives a similar impression to the final scene of *The Pillars of the Community*. The admission made, all seems clear and easily borne: but what of Miss Lucy's hopeless love, and how is Consul Bernick to go on living, conscious of his crimes? Even an only moderately sceptical reader feels, in each case, some doubts as to the future of the personalities thus depicted.

However, even at this early stage, it was not usual for Freud to expect a rapid liquidation of hysteria. In the majority of cases, it is made plain in the 'Preliminary Communication', mere elucidation is not enough; rather the effect must be abreacted: abreaction, strictly speaking, takes place in practical terms, for example in acts of revenge, but it may also occur vicariously, through verbal expression or the manifestation of emotion. This is what Freud and Breuer, taking the name from a celebrated passage in Aristotle's *Poetics*, called the 'cathartic method'. Freud had a particular reason for being interested in the Aristotelian notion of catharsis since an uncle of his wife, the scholarly Professor Jakob Bernays of Bonn, had made this the subject of a special study. According to Bernays it would be a false interpretation of Aristotle to consider catharsis - as many aestheticians have done - as a purification *through* the emotions. What Aristotle had meant was a purification *of* the emotions; after the performance the audience could go on their way relieved, liberated from the pressure of sentiments, for the emotions were discharged in watching the drama. Bernays is able to support this view (among others) by citing Iamblichus, the neoplatonist author of *De Mysteriis*, whose explanations accord, point for point, with the early psychoanalytic conception of the course of a cathartic process:

> If we wish wholly to hold in check the powers which in us become general human affections, they grow all the stronger. If, on the other hand, we were to draw them forth in brief and duly measured utterances, they would gain a certain tempered joy, they would of their own accord, without restraint, be calmed, relieved and mitigated. Hence, by comedy as well as tragedy, we are accustomed through the spectacle of others' emotions to still our own affections, to make them more measured and to relieve them; and likewise we also free ourselves in the temples through seeing and hearing certain impure things which would bring hurt if practiced in truth.[13]

Breuer and Freud understood the notion of catharsis in this 'medical' sense. This meant, to take the comparison with Ibsen a step further, a considerable deepening of the conception as compared with the intellectualist-moralist viewpoint that appears in *The Pillars of the Community*. But Freud assuredly also knew the Ibsen who, later, wrote such plays as *Rosmersholm, The Wild Duck* and *The Lady from The Sea*. Ibsen was by then not so certain that the liberation from the 'vital lie' brings harmony or that the truth brings relief; at the same time, as the focus shifts from the social to the psychological relationships the conclusions become increasingly pessimistic. After the great reconciliations and all the revelations in *Rosmersholm*, Rosmer and Rebekka have learned to understand each other better than before; henceforth mutual understanding marks their relations. But, as Rebekka sees it, insight brings with it only a stronger sense of guilt: '. . . *that's* the dreadful thing, that now, when all the happiness of life is offered me with full hands - I'm changed, so that my own past bars my way'.[14] When, in the end, the pair die together, the witness, Madame Helseth says: 'The dead mistress has taken them.'[15] She might equally have said: 'The past has taken them.'

'*Hysterics suffer mainly from reminiscences.*' In Breuer and Freud's 'Preliminary Communication'[16] this sentence on the cathartic method is printed in italics. The same remark might be made of many of Ibsen's characters. But whilst in his earlier socially-critical plays, Ibsen allows his characters the chance of liberating themselves from the past simply with the aid of the will and the intellectual faculties, he seems later to consider them as given over almost entirely to the tyranny of memories. Freud could not adopt either of these points of view. His determinism, the pessimism to which he alludes in the letter to Schnitzler already quoted, must have drawn him to the standpoints of the later Ibsen; on the other hand his rationalist and radical attitude must have aroused his sympathies with the earlier one. As a medical man he was compelled to take the middle course: at all times he was apprehensive of underestimating the therapeutic difficulties, yet at all times too he remained confident in the power of the conscious to put all things in order and in the possibility, through abreaction, of relieving pathological pressures. His essay on *Rosmersholm* might, from this point of view, almost be taken as a call for restraint in face of Ibsen's radical pessimism; if the *dénouement* of the play is so tragic, this is because the characters have not fully carried out their own psychoanalysis, and Freud completes this by uncovering, by psychological means, layers of guilt more ancient than Rebekka and Rosmer have themselves revealed.

But Ibsen and Freud can on occasion meet half way. The first time Ibsen surprised his public by adding an 'expressive question-mark' to his hypermoral cult of the truth was in *The Wild Duck*, the starting-point of a ten-year discussion of the *raison d'être* of the 'vital lie'. Hjalmar Ekdal had woven a web of illusions to escape from his humiliating position of suppliant *vis-à-vis* the wholesale merchant Werle, and to convince himself in imagination that he is a man of consequence; as Ingjald Nissen has shown, this is the stock image of the neurotic according to the Adlerian school of individual psychology.[17] When Gregers Werle intervenes and reveals to him the truth about his life, catastrophe results for the family; and Ekdal himself does not seem prepared to accept the truth. Whether or not this is Ibsen's intention, the majority of audiences seem inclined to see the drama as an illustration of Dr Relling's thesis: 'Take the saving lie from the average man and you take his happiness away, too.'[18] Freud's method is directed towards teaching men the truth about themselves, but he cannot but reflect upon the problem of Ibsen's 'saving lie', and on occasion he has been able to answer the question wholly in the spirit of Dr Relling. Thus he was able in the *Introductory Lectures* to write of the 'flight into illness', that is, of the Ekdal syndrome:

> Indeed there are cases in which even the physician must admit that for a conflict to end in neurosis is the most harmless and socially tolerable solution. You must not be surprised to hear that even the physician may occasionally take the side of the illness he is combating. It is not his business to restrict himself in every situation in life to being a fanatic in favour of health. He knows that there is not only neurotic misery in the world but real, irremovable suffering as well, that necessity may even require a person to sacrifice his health; and he learns that a sacrifice of this kind made by a single person can prevent immeasurable unhappiness for many others. If we may say, then, that whenever a neurotic is faced by a conflict he takes flight into illness, yet we must allow that in some cases that flight is fully justified, and a physician who has recognized how the situation lies will silently and solicitously withdraw.[19]

In his work of the 1880s Ibsen poses in a most marked way a problem which, for him, was always acute and personal - that of the liberty of the individual personality. He saw the individual as shackled in all manner of restrictive social conventions. How could he rid himself of this restrictive heritage and become a 'new' man? Could he ever free himself from 'ghosts'? Sometimes Ibsen appears to give a negative answer to this question, sometimes he inclines to a more optimistic conception. Freud takes up the problem from Ibsen, but at the same time freeing it from all social philosophy and isolating the psychological aspect. For Freud the crucial thing was to free men from the burden of their past and, in so doing, to make them autonomous personalities. And, like Ibsen, Freud swung between confidence and resignation as regards the therapeutic possibilities.

It was all the easier for Freud to interiorize the problems in so far as he could follow in Ibsen's footsteps. Towards the end of the 1880s Ibsen's work itself came to a turning-point. Radical criticism of society lost for him something of its urgency, and at the same time he began to take an interest in hypnotism and suggestion, in the 'night side of the soul', that was a characteristic interest of the naturalism of the period. This does not by any means signify that he ceased to be concerned with the problem of liberty. On the contrary, the question of the free man is as central as ever. The three 'psychopathological' dramas - *Rosmersholm, The Lady from the Sea* and *Hedda Gabler* - are every bit as concerned with the liberation of man from his oppressive past. Halvdan Koht has put this clearly in respect of the first of these plays:

> Rosmer's story is once more the story of Mrs Alving, the basic theme that Ibsen repeated from his youth: the past, living in the present, capable of avenging itself at any moment. In Mrs Alving the struggle is against the past as it appears in the ideas ingrained by education and social custom;

in Rosmer the struggle is against the legacy of the past in his own temperament. The problem is unresolved in *Ghosts*; now Ibsen probes to a far deeper psychological level and follows Rosmer's struggle through to the end - an end which must come in death, since the 'white horses' prove to be invincible.[20]

The end of *Hedda Gabler* is as tragic as that of *Rosmersholm*. Like Rosmer and like Madame Alving, Hedda Gabler - the daughter of a general - dreams of a freer life, symbolized by the recurring phrase 'with vineleaves in the hair';[21] but her education has erected barriers about her which she never succeeds in breaking down. She is thereby condemned to live as a parasite upon others; hysterically: when she realizes that they have no need of her, nothing remains for her but to commit suicide. In the background (as with Strindberg's *Miss Julie*) one can discern a horror of sexuality, the consequence of the grotesque education of young girls 'of good family'. Norwegian criticism pays particular attention to this *motif* and Koht characterizes the portrait of Hedda as 'a perfect example of the kind of problem which twentieth-century psychoanalysts would examine'.[22] To this we may appropriately add that the young Freud in the *Studies on Hysteria* commented in similar vein when he wrote that the peasant girl, Katherina, had 'made it so much easier for me to talk to her than to the prudish ladies of my city practice, who regard whatever is natural as shameful'.[23]

There are numerous points of similarity between Hedda Gabler and Freud's female patients. But if one wishes to lay stress upon the play that, among Ibsen's pathological dramas, corresponds most closely to

Freud's ideas on the life of the psyche, it is not *Hedda Gabler* that first springs to mind. Neither for Freud nor for Ibsen at this time was the sickness of the soul unreservedly to be explained in terms of an unsuitable education or oppressive social conventions. In both cases this is, rather, a secondary *motif*. The deeper psychological aspect is revealed far more clearly in *The Lady from the Sea*, a play situated in the middle of the series of psychological dramas. As the Norwegian psychoanalist Ragnar Vogt has emphasized, we are confronted here with 'a first-rate example of a psychoanalytic cure'.[24]

The play was published in 1888 and performed the following year in the writer's homeland and in Germany. The interest Ibsen aroused was at this time reaching its summit. In Germany the great Ibsen controversy was still raging, reinforced by the police ban on performances of *Ghosts*, which lasted from 1886 to 1888. This struggle for Ibsen was no less violent than the struggle for Freud in the twentieth century. More than any other, Ibsen was the symbol of intrepid truthfulness and when, towards the end of the 1880s, victory was within reach, it was - in Germany, at all events - the most notable triumph of 'modern' ideas.

But Ibsen meanwhile was absorbed with psychological problems which now and then confounded his partisans, without conservative public opinion being thereby at all mollified. This was the reason, despite his worldwide reputation and despite his being the watchword of the 'moderns', for the mixed reception accorded to his new works. The reaction to *The Lady from the Sea* was especially hesitant. Ellida Wangel, Koht writes, was considered 'a peculiar psychiatric case',[25] and the play as a whole aroused more bafflement than comprehension. Brandes devoted only a few lines to it in his book on Ibsen, but he described it as 'a very skilfully carried out psychologico-fantastic experiment'.[26] Litzmann, an admirer of Ibsen, writing in 1901, was severe in his judgement on this piece; according to him it was 'inwardly false, because merely put together'.[27] Koht maintains that it was not until the centenary celebrations of 1928 that the work was successfully presented - 'what struck one after so many years was the play's modernity and its close relation to recent psychological theories, particularly those of Pierre Janet, developed in the 1890s, and of Sigmund Freud, from the same period - although given general circulation only in the early years of the twentieth century'.[28]

This is a situation that calls for particular caution in the interpretation of *The Lady from the Sea.* Whoever now reads the play or sees it performed has the impression of sitting in on a psychoanalysis, brilliantly cast in dramatic form. But it is abundantly clear that in approaching the work in this manner we run the risk of reading into the drama ideas originating in the Freudian school which would, perhaps, be alien to its author.

There were, however, in the 1890s, those who in principle could have regarded this play of Ibsen's in the same way as we do today. One of those best qualified to understand its psychological message was Arthur Schnitzler in his double role of physician specializing in hypnosis and connoisseur of erotic entanglements. When he wrote his *Paracelsus* (already referred to) he based it on a theme fundamentally similar to that of *The Lady from the Sea.* Schnitzler describes how, under hypnotic treatment, the modest Justina abandons herself to a long-forgotten youthful love. But the idea is not, of course, that this dangerous undercurrent has been created by the hypnosis; it has been there all the time, under the superficialities of bourgeois correctitude. Ellida Wangel undergoes a similar experience; she is living with an intelligent and understanding man to whom she is faithfully married, but when the stranger comes on the scene she feels herself subjected to the whole power of a demoniacal attraction she thought had been overcome.

If we wish to know to what extent the psychological penetration in Ibsen's drama is conscious, we must turn first to the secondary characters, for example to Ellida's adolescent stepdaughter, Hilde Wangel. Her portrait is very finely etched and in such a way that it is only by degrees that the audience realizes the ambivalences of her inner life. When she first appears on the scene, it seems as if she detests her stepmother even more than her elder sister, but when, at the end of the drama, Ellida threatens to leave them it is Hilde and not Bolette who is desolated. Ibsen has depicted in every bit as delicate a manner how she takes pity on the tubercular Lyngstrand; perhaps she is to some extent in love with him: but she conceals her sentiments behind a mask of teasing flippancy. With great finesse, Ibsen makes it clear that she and her sister, along with Dr Wangel, have practised a cult of their dead mother's memory, by means of which Ellida has been excluded from the intimacy of the family circle. The character of Lyngstrand is likewise based on psychological observation - of the self-deceiving optimism of the terminal sufferer from tuberculosis. Doctor Wangel himself is one of Ibsen's clearest and most sympathetic portraits: the faithful husband who conceals his unhappiness and withdraws into the background, who is not without his weaknesses but, in the last analysis, shows himself to have insight and good intentions.

In this self-sufficient network of fixed psychological relationships, Ellida Wangel is the dominating personality. Independently of any symbolic significance that might be attributed to her as 'The Lady from the Sea', it is *a priori* probable that Ibsen was concerned with the psychological verisimilitude of the portrait. Ibsen himself provides a sort of key to her character in the conversation in the fourth act between Wangel and his friend Arnholm. Ellida is ill, Wangel says, but hers is 'not ordinary illness' such as can be cured with 'any ordinary medicine'.[29] Her unpredictability, her changes of mood, her lack of contact with others derive from her coming of 'seafaring stock' whose moods vary with the ebb and flow of the waves. Fundamentally her restlessness does not depend on the news that her former fiancée, the sailor, is on his way home - 'that's another thing she may have imagined, or persuaded herself into, since the day before yesterday'.[30] 'Signs of it had been noticeable long before'; indeed on that occasion she had had 'rather a severe attack'.[31] It was at this point, a member of the audience may add, that she broke off marital relations with Dr Wangel.

This whole line of reasoning takes medical elements as its point of departure and, with certain modifications, could equally well figure in the case notes of a psychiatric illness. If it is not the whole truth about Ellida, it is at all events a pointer to an important part of that truth. Seen in this sober light the fantasies about the man from the sea, the child's eyes and the milky pearl in the tiepin are no more than neurotic symbols of the deep cleavage in Ellida's psyche. According to Wangel's interpretation Ellida lived, like Freud's neurotics, in a dream world where illusion and truth mingle, and the dominant principle is the conflict between the conscious, well-directed ego and the dangerous subconscious impulses.

What above all throws doubts on this 'rational' view is the entry of the 'stranger' in the fifth act. He plays a decisive role in Ellida's fantasy world; his image, set against a marine background, is bound up with the general theme of erotic liberty. With his entry on the scene, a materialization takes place, Ellida's dream suddenly takes on physical form. In terms of the construction of the play, some such development was inevitable. Ellida must choose between her unhealthy fantasy world and the reality Dr Wangel represents. She could have explained her choice as something that happened *within* her - as a patient might, on being cured - but that would not have constituted the final scene of a play: the choice must be concretized before the eyes of the audience. On the other hand the 'stranger' must not become so 'real' that Ellida becomes simply a woman choosing between two lovers; that would have made nonsense of the play as a *problem* play. Ibsen must have sensed this difficulty and thus resolved to present the 'stranger' as a being not quite either phantom or man. He has him behave, to say the least, somewhat oddly, as if acting in a dream, and hints that at first Wangel had difficulty in seeing him; but of course as the conversation between the three progresses, so he becomes more 'real' to the audience. This device (which is not entirely successful) lends the whole drama an equivocal character, and it is an easy matter to question whether other elements one has taken for Ellida's unhealthy fantasies (as for example her declaration that the child has 'eyes that change colour with the sea') do not also have a certain mystical reality. All things considered, Ibsen was not perhaps at all unopposed to such uncertainties.

But if one opts for a purely psychological under-

standing of the work, the *dénouement* of the drama fits
comfortably with the rest. Ellida is compelled to make
a free choice, and the secret temptations the stranger
from the sea symbolizes thus loose their attraction. In
reality the choice does not concern the stranger but
what he represents in her inner world, her dimly
glimpsed instinctive impulses. 'The terrible thing' she
declares 'lies deeper, Wangel ... it is the terrible
fascination in my own mind';[32] and Wangel returns to
this idea in the decisive scene: 'I'm slowly beginning to
understand you. You think and reason in pictures - in
visual images. This longing of yours - this yearning for
the sea, and the fascination that *he* - this stranger - had
for you, were really only the expression of a new and
growing urge in you for freedom. ... That's all.'[33]

What Wangel and Ellida accomplish in their great
dialogue - and what corresponds to the scenes of
'unburdening' in many of Ibsen's dramas - is a
'reworking' of the past and, at the same time, a clarifica-
tion of Ellida's unconscious desires, concealed as they
are in 'pictures' and 'visual images'. They are participat-
ing in a therapeutic conversation of the same sort as
Freud employed with his patients at the beginning of
the 1890s. As with them, the decisive realities prove to
be exclusively determined by the psyche - what happened in the past or might still happen is of minor
importance compared with the living notion of the
past in men's minds: in both cases the intentions of the
*unconscious* must be deciphered from the symbolic language it employs. Wangel plays the role of an analyst;
and it is not without reason that Ellida affirms: 'But
you have been a good doctor to me.'[34]

Ellida's way takes her through a crisis to health.
When everything that had been troubling her for all
those years takes on a concrete form, her reactions

assume a more violent character than hitherto, but, at the same time she can accept it or reject it - the choice has become possible. She prefers to reject it and in so doing she triumphs over the temptation that was forcing her to separate from her family, threatening to drive her 'into the unknown'.[35] In comparison with the *dénouement* of *Rosmersholm* or *Hedda Gabler*, this is a 'happy ending', a happy ending in the same sense as an analysis brought to a successful conclusion. Freud would not, to be sure, have spoken so solemnly about 'freedom' and 'responsibility' as Wangel does in the last act[36] - he was too much of a determinist for that - but he would not have overlooked the parallel between Ellida's recovery and the 'cathartic' effect he himself expected from his treatments.

Most likely there was no 'Lady from the Sea' among Freud's patients; in the nature of things there cannot have been many in the Dual Monarchy. His own experience of the sea was negligible. Nonetheless, as Alf Kjéllen has shown,[37] water symbolism plays an important role in Freud's doctrine. Dreams of the sea are interpreted primarily as dreams of birth (the breaking of the waters!), but at the same time, it is pointed out, constitute an 'ancestral' memory of the epoch in which man's predecessors led an aquatic life - this last supposition being based on a hypothesis of Haeckel's, who also had an influence on Ibsen at the time when he took up the theme of *The Lady from the Sea*. Water, ultimately, is linked as a *motif* with the longing for a pre-human state, a return to the pre-human states of existence, a state free of consciousness and responsibility, indeed with a death instinct. In *The Lady from the Sea* this symbolism is closely associated with, indeed assimilated to, that of the 'black soundless wings' that will carry Ellida off 'into the darkness'.[38]

Direct evidence is lacking as to what Freud thought of Ibsen's 'psychoanalytic' dramas.[39] But we may be certain that, in one way or another, he was aware of them; Ibsen's position in the German-speaking world was such that a man of Freud's sort could not have avoided hearing of a new work of his. *The Lady from the Sea* was published at a time when Freud was preparing definitively to pass over into the field of psychotherapy, and thus at a period when he must have been especially responsive to stimulating new ideas. The similarities between Ibsen's mode of thinking in *The Lady from the Sea* - and also, to a lesser extent in the two other psychopathological dramas - and Freud's methods are, when all is said and done, so great that it is only with difficulty that one can describe them as merely fortuitous parallels. Until such time as new materials comes to light, it seems plausible to consider the Ibsen of *The Lady from the Sea* as one of the minds that gave stimulus to Freud's imagination.

But the problem should not (and need not) be left to one side without first drawing attention to a deeper parallelism which can explain how it came about that Freud, as a psychotherapist, could learn from Ibsen the dramatist. Both were of course influenced by the revived interest in individual psychology, in 'the secrets of the soul', an interest which is one of the hallmarks of so much of the literature and of the 'mental set' of the *fin-de-siècle*. Over and above that however each was in his way part of another and more specific tradition - that of 'the analytical drama'.

By 'the analytical drama' Schiller - who is said to have coined the phrase - meant those plays in which the dramatic development consists of a step-by-step unveiling of the hidden secrets of the past. Thus, inevitably, the analytic drama is a drama concerned with the past and the present. In it the crucial question is always whether the protagonists will be able to cope with, to overcome and subsume their own past and thereby create for themselves a new life. In *The Lady from the Sea* this outcome seems probable; but in many analytical dramas - such as the prototype of the genre, *Oedipus Rex* - the only solution is to draw bitter conclusions from what has happened long ago. In other plays by Ibsen - for example in *Ghosts* - the past is presented as a hereditary taint or, as in *Rosmersholm*, an unavowed crime rather than a divine judgement. But it remains the past: it cannot be undone, and its power is terrible.

When we come to consider Freud the psychotherapist there are numerous indications that the analytical drama (and more specifically *Oedipus Rex*) was more or less constantly at the back of his mind during the formative years of his career. There are frequent references to the classical world of myth and tragedy and, what is more important, they 'come to the surface', as it were, at the most strategic moments in the development of Freud's thinking. In this way, as has already been pointed out, Freud's early discovery of the healing power of insight into things past took its name in his writings - the cathartic effect - from Aristotle's *Poetics*, in which the analytical drama of *Oedipus Rex* is the principal *explanandum*. And again, when Freud subsequently thought he had identified the most important and ominous of the ties that are embedded in the past, the root of difficulties in later life, he borrowed the name of Sophocles' tragic hero and called his discovery the Oedipus complex. From this we may presume that he believed he had found something in actual life that was just as important, just as fateful as the hidden events of Sophocles' play were for King Oedipus.

All this might well be take as fortuitous were it not for Freud's sly, almost secretive way of letting drop such clues to the less scientific side of his thinking. Seen in this light the very specific references to the classical drama take on a deeper significance when one reflects on the manifest similarities between the 'procedure', the 'development' in the analytical drama and in Freud's theory in its mature form. In Freud's 'therapeutic drama' with its two protagonists, the patient is of course the hero; the therapist is his assistant and has the same task as Tiresias (or the messenger) in the play: that of helping him discover his past. This was already the case in the *Studies on Hysteria*. But to Freud discovery in itself became insufficient and he introduced a specifically dramatic element into his scenario when he laid bare the crisis that follows upon the discovery, later to be called the 'transference situation', in which the therapist is drawn into the action as an object of hatred or love. This of course corresponds to the well-known dramatic situation in which the hero threatens to kill the messenger (or the prophet) who tells him the truth. But it also corresponds to what Aristotelian dramatic theory calls a *peripeteia*, a turning-point from which the drama proceeds to a tragic or a (relatively) happy ending.

This story of dramatic situation is directly comparable to that of *The Lady from the Sea*. Whether or not Freud had actually read the play does not greatly matter. The obvious parallels can be explained in terms of similar starting-points - in terms of the preoccupation with psychology and the analytical drama that Ibsen and Freud shared. When at a later date J.L. Moreno, one of Freud's less-well-known followers created the 'psychodrama' as a more organized form of dramatic therapy he was merely taking up and further developing the dramatic elements inherent in Freud's conception.

# VI   Man naturally mad

IN the course of the *Introductory Lectures*, Freud compares his own contribution to those of Copernicus and Darwin. 'The naïve self-love of men' he says, 'has had to submit to two major blows.'[1] The first of these took place when he realized that our earth was not the central point of the universe.

> The second blow fell when biological research destroyed man's supposedly privileged place in creation and proved his descent from the animal kingdom and his ineradicable animal nature. This revaluation has been accomplished in our own days by Darwin, Wallace and their predecessors, though not without the most violent contemporary opposition. But human megalomania will have suffered its third and most wounding blow from the psychological research of the present time which seems to prove to the ego that it is not even master in its own house, but must content itself with scanty information: information of what is going on unconsciously in its mind. ... Hence arises the general revolt against our science, the disregard of all considerations of academic civility and the releasing of the opposition from every restraint of impartial logic.[2]

The resemblances between the reactions to Darwin's doctrine of origins and the reception accorded to Freud's psychoanalysis are striking. They do not merely concern the simple fact that in each case a theory, presented as purely scientific, became the subject of dispute well beyond the confines of the world of learning. The lines followed by the discussions were also in many respects similar. Both Darwin and Freud challenged religious beliefs, but at the same time an act of quasi-religious faith was needed on the part of their partisans. Darwin's central idea, that of natural selection, is not, any more than is Freud's idea of the unconscious, something open to conclusive demonstration; in each case it is a question of hypotheses appearing to acquire a greater credibility as elements of experience are amassed which seem to testify in their favour. But given that the new elements are constantly interpreted in the light of the hypotheses which must be demonstrated, a sceptic can never be wholly convinced of their truth. Both Darwin and Freud figure today among the great names in the annals of science, but nonetheless this does not prevent certain persons from still regarding their hypotheses as being essentially defective. By their very method they have given rise to a dialogue which could, in principle, be continued to eternity.

This parallelism is not an effect of chance. The Darwinian revolution was the immediate condition for the psychology of Freud. Freud had, in our view, incorporated a great deal of Darwin's standpoint into his system. Furthermore it is more than probable that he had the intention, more or less conscious, of provoking in the realm of psychology the same upheaval that Darwin had done in the realm of biology.

Freud was, it goes without saying, a Darwinian in his biological conceptions. He had already come to know in his schooldays of the new doctrine which, in those days, was occupying the minds of all Europe. Later, as a researcher, he fell under the influence of the physiologist von Brücke - the man who, as Freud himself attests, had the greatest influence on his intellectual orientation. It was through him that he became acquainted with the principles of evolution in his laboratory work. As he recounts in the *Introductory Lectures*, it was under Brücke's direction that he began the study of the nerve fibres of a certain fish, and he discovered that in the course of evolution its nerve cells had migrated from one part of the organism to another, in such a way that some had remained behind on the way.[3]

The example was presented as a 'parallel' of the sexual development of man which, according to Freud, might take place in such a way that certain elements might evolve normally while others remain at a previous stage. It is only natural to suppose the mechanism of evolution, as understood by the Darwinians, served Freud as a model for his thinking when he conceived his theory of sex. It is likewise apparent that his presentation of the ego and of sexual evolution derive from one of Darwin's favourite ideas. The evolution of the ego and, similarly, of the libido, Freud states towards the end of the *Introductory Lectures*, '[are] both . . . at bottom heritages, abbreviated recapitulations of the development which all mankind has passed through from its primaeval days over long periods of time'.[4]

In adhering to this theory Freud was adhering to Haeckel's 'biogenetic law', according to which the development of the individual recapitulates the development of the species - 'ontogeny recapitulates phylogeny'. This particularly exciting aspect was the contribution of the foremost German exponent of Darwinism: if the biogenetic law were valid, then each one of us could trace out in his own being the prehistory of all humanity. For Freud, as also for his pupil C.G. Jung, this was the point of departure for a series of audacious speculations. From the earliest days of psychoanalysis the idea was with Freud as a borrowing, without further elaboration, from Darwinism. In *The Interpretation of Dreams, à propos* of regression it is stated that 'behind this childhood of the individual we are promised a picture of a phylogenetic childhood - a picture of the development of the human race, of which the individual's development is in fact an abbreviated recapitulation influenced by the chance circumstances of life'.[5] Psychoanalysis can thus claim 'a high place among the sciences which are concerned with the reconstruction of the earliest and most obscure periods of the beginnings of the human race'.[6]

It is only in later editions of *The Interpreation of Dreams* that these speculative visions make their appearance, but allusions to Freud's archaeological leanings and his passionate interest in human prehistory already exist in the first edition. In one of Freud's dreams of the period - one which is also concerned with a (still unwritten) 'immortal work' of his own - Rider Haggard's novel *She* is involved.[7] *She* is a novel of adventure, telling of an archaeological expedition in Africa, trekking across a boggy landscape to uncover age-old secrets hitherto hidden from humanity. Without seeking to exercise Freud's prerogative as an interpreter of dreams, one may suppose that this pretty run-of-the-mill novel might well have interested him, given that in the period of his first psychoanalytical researches he felt himself to be like an explorer in a boggy landscape, seeking out the great secrets of humanity.

Even when the 'biogenetic' implications are laid to one side, Freud's doctrine of regression bears traces of its Darwinian origin. According to the definition in *The Interpretation of Dreams*, regression is that process whereby the dreamer shifts from the higher, more complex psychic levels to ones more primitive and simple and, at the same time, revives for example memories of childhood. The underlying structure of Freudian thinking, centred on the mechanism of development, is here clearly apparent. On the strength of what Spencer called 'levels of integration' the later stages of development are regarded as 'higher', and the dream work - like the neurotic functions - is considered as a relapse to past stages, a sort of atavism. In an analogous manner, according to Haeckel, the head-stripes of a quagga may appear in a domesticated horse - the 'souvenir' of millennia of evolution.

When Freud formed his image of the life of the psyche, with its tension between the unconscious, governed by the instincts, and the ego, erected by society, he already set out from Darwinian presuppositions. In so doing he gave a full orchestration to a theme well known in the Darwinian writings of the turn of the century; with Zola, we might call this theme 'the beast in man'. In his novel *La Bête humaine*, Zola tells the story of an engine driver, Lantier, who is seized by a pathological urge to kill and murders his mistress. According to Zola this is a 'regression': Lantier wishes to revenge himself, on behalf of the entire male sex, for all the injustices it has had to undergo since prehistoric times. Atavistic instincts take possession of him and compel him to the deed against his will. In a more psychologically refined guise we come on the same conception of man's position, between the primitive and civilization, in Bourget's well-known *Le Disciple* (1889), which is presented as being written by a young murderer. Just how close the literary psychology of the *fin de siècle* comes to Freud's fundamental intuitions is clearly shown by Brandes in his essay 'The Beast in Man':

What is developed in the story is, above all, the doubling, in the simplest sense, of the self. The self is part conscious, part unconscious. This, in general, explains life's errors and misconceptions. There is within us a universe of which we are unaware, of which we never know anything, save perhaps that it is the precise opposite of what we believe we are. From this follows those very shifts or reversals in feeling and behaviour we observe or experience. For example a man will work for some aim upon which he believes his happiness depends and, when he achieves his goal, realize that he has misconstrued the true but secret promptings of his inner life. Another appears like other men and acts as others do. All at once the image of his misfortunes rises up before him, a constant anxiety, a constant danger he had striven to forget, that suddenly overwhelms him and could give his life a completely different direction.[8]

But it is not only as a psychologist of the instincts that Freud finds himself in agreement with the common conceptions of the post-Darwinians and the naturalists. Darwinism has sometimes also been called a transformism, and indeed it sets out in the long run to demonstrate how species are transformed under the pressure of circumstances. Freud applied an analogous notion of transformism to the life of the psyche. Unconscious impulses are such that they cannot assert themselves under their original form; but they have a charge of psychic energy which makes it impossible for them to be completely suppressed. For this reason they present themselves in transformed shapes, in dreams or as neurotic symptoms, adapted to the conditions of life that the censorship and social controls have, so to speak, dictated. This mechanism resembles what the Darwinists have called 'mimicry'. If an aphis takes on a green colouring by way of camouflage, this is an unconscious strategy - just as when one of Freud's patients conceals murderous desires towards one of his closest kin under the mask of an innocent symbol.

So readily were its methods carried over to a field other than that of biology, that Darwinism could stimulate exertions at a further, even more central, point. Darwin's special contribution to the theory of evolution certainly lies first and foremost in his having established the concept of a 'struggle for existence' as a causal explanation of development. He marked himself off thereby from those who were happy enough to accept the idea of evolution as such, but who looked upon it as a supplementary proof of the 'natural order'. For Darwin development was governed by a self-regulating mechanism. In terms of theory, he arrived at this idea by rejecting the idea of the closed unity of species as conceived by Linnaeus; for him individuals were primary, and he conceived them as being in conflict one with another. In and through this struggle the species is formed and develops the characteristics that are valuable for its continuance. What had hitherto appeared as the mark of constancy and similitude, dissolves under Darwin's scrutiny into an immense diversity of variants which, in the internecine struggle, become the weapons of the individual. Upon closer examination 'fitness' appears to be a covert equilibrium of antagonistic forces.

Such a way of thinking was in many ways attractive. It seemed empirically reassuring: what could be more realistic than to explain great events by an immense number of minute causes? It also provided an explanation of 'fitness' in nature, but had pitiless struggle as its background. Perhaps to some degree it also corresponded to the individualism of the liberal epoch. At all events it is beyond doubt that Darwin's method was contagious and was soon applied in domains unknown to him.

Transposing to the organism itself the conceptions that Darwin had applied to species and to the relations between organisms, Wilhelm Roux, a student of Haeckel's, laid the basis for what has been called the mechanism of evolution. The 'fitness' of the organism may also be explained, in Haeckel's terms, according to the principle of selection; not however in Darwin's sense whereby the struggle for existence is carried on between individuals, but in the sense that a constant struggle for existence rages between all the parts of the individual organism. In the first instance Haeckel would have been inclined to speak of a 'selection of individuals', in the second, of a 'selection of cells'.[9]

It is evident that provided the subject-matter could be broken up into smaller units, sufficiently numerous and sufficiently discrete, this mode of thinking could be used at any desired level. Applied to psychology, this conception assured a solid grounding to the sensualist and associationist schools of thought and made a clean sweep of notions of the unity of the self or of the personality. The idea found its most explicit form in Hippolyte Taine's great philosophical work *On Intelligence* (1870), a work which in its turn inspired other French psychologists such as Ribot and Janet. Freud had read Taine's work by about 1896 and wrote to Fliess: 'Taine's book ... gives me especial satisfaction.'[10] But he would already have been able in many ways to become acquainted with the basic ideas involved.

Taine's learned treatise is concerned not only with questions of psychology but also with the problems of epistemology: it calls to mind the works of Spinoza and Condillac as well as other philosophical authorities. But when the question arises of his fundamental view of the life of the psyche, Taine openly avows his dependence on Darwin, a dependence which is not confined to the idea of evolution and the biological struggle for existence, but extends to the Darwinian method as described above. Taine writes in a note on the 'struggle for life': 'The theory of the great English naturalist is nowhere more precisely applicable than in psychology.'[11]

From the start Taine takes up the idea as it was developed by Roux in respect of the cells of the organism. The same holds, he maintains, in psychology:

> All that observation detects psychologically in the thinking being are, in addition to sensations, images of different kinds, primitive or consecutive, endued with certain tendencies, and modified in their development by the concurrence or antagonism of other simultaneous or contiguous images. Just as the living body is a polypus of mutually dependent cells, so the active mind is a polypus of mutually dependent sensations and images, and in the one case as in the other, unity is nothing more than a harmony and an effect. Every image is possessed of an automatic force, and tends spontaneously to a particular state; to hallucination, false recollection, and other illusions of madness. But it is arrested in its progress by the contradiction of a sensation, of another image, or group of images. The mutual arrest, the reciprocal clash, produce by their combined effect

an equilibrium; and the effect we have just seen produced by the special corrective sensation, by the connexion of our recollections, by the order of our general judgements, is but an instance of the constant re-arrangement and incessant limitation which innumerable incompatibilities and conflicts are incessantly bringing about in our images and ideas. This equilibrium is the state of reasonable wakefulness. As soon as it is at an end by the hypertrophy or atrophy of an element, we are mad, wholly or partially. When it lasts over a certain time, the fatigue is too great, and we sleep; our images are no longer reduced and guided by antagonistic sensations coming from the outer world, by the repressive effect of combined recollections, by the dominion of well-connected judgements; so they then acquire their full development, turn into hallucinations, arrange themselves spontaneously according to new tendencies, and sleep, though crowded with intense dreams, is a rest, since, suppressing a constraint, it brings on a state of relaxation.[12]

This *resumé* of Taine's conception of psychology - the doctrine, as Paul Rubow has characterized it, of *l'homme naturellement fou*[13] - constitutes an important stage in the development of naturalist psychology and thereby situates it in the development of Freud. Its dynamic aspect differentiates it from the old associationist psychology. The antagonism between the ideas, the 'images', is underlined here in a manner more evident than in Herbart, who is often mentioned in connection with the formation of Freud's first theories. Each idea strives to rise to the surface of the 'reservoir' of memories to which it has been consigned, and would dominate the consciousness at the expense of the others.[14] The normal functioning of the life of the psyche appears as a precarious equilibrium which holds in check and even suppresses the most troublesome ideas. In dreams and in abnormal states they take their revenge: the personality then emerges in its state of original chaos.

With such a point of departure, for the psychologist abnormal states become a more interesting subject of study than the acquired equilibrium of daily life, the dream more fruitful than the waking state, the division of the personality more revealing than the self that has contrived to preserve its identity. Psychology becomes in essence the study of psychopathology. When Ribot studies the disorders of the personality, when, at the same time as Breuer and Freud, Janet interests himself in the traumatic recollections of hysteria, they are taking the direction pointed out by Taine. But the latter had already assembled an imposing documentation of the irregular states in which the life of the psyche appeared in all its primal disorganization. He took a particular interest in the phenomena of the 'doubling' of the personality, and one may see an indication of the affinity between naturalist-Darwinian psychology and emergent psychoanalysis in the fact that Breuer's famous case, that of Anna O., which gave rise to the idea of the cathartic method, was precisely a case of the hysterical doubling of the personality.

Freud became aware of Taine's work at a time when he must have been particularly open to impressions. At the beginning of 1896 his work on hysteria lay behind him, and he was on the verge of going over definitively to psychology, or rather to psychology set against a philosophical background of what he called 'metapsychology'. The correspondence with Fliess

testifies to a feverish activity and a constant exchange
of speculative ideas. The 'self-analysis' and the work
on dreams lay in the immediate future. Freud fanta-
sized of writing a massive synthetic account of the
neuroses, but at the same time he admitted to not
having to hand all the materials he needed. At times he
still spoke in the language of the physiologist, on other
occasions he tried to bring his observations into line
with the biological speculations of Fliess. It is only
natural that, in this agitated and productive period, he
should have studied *De l'Intelligence* with interest. In
it he found a synthesis every bit as grandiose as that he
dreamed of. In it too he found brilliant formulations
bearing on the experiences he had encountered in his
studies of hysteria - as, for example, when Taine
speaks of the human brain as being like 'a theatre
where many plays are being simultaneously performed, on many stages, only one of which is lit'.[15]

In Taine's system 'reduction' plays a role analogous
to that later played by 'censorship' in Freud's theory of
dreams. An idea thrusts itself forward, seeking to
develop into a hallucination, but meets with another
idea which 'reduces' the first and compels it to return
to the subconscious. The decisive factor about 'reduct-
ives' and the 'censorship' is the necessity for a rational
adaptation to the external restrictions of life - a Darwinian idea which Freud later took up again and
reworked to establish his 'reality principle'.

Neither for Taine nor for Freud is there, in the long
run, any problem in explaining mental illness or abnormal states: in different ways they reflect the primal conflicts in the human psyche. The problem is rather to
explain the possibility of a rational adaptation in the
normal man. Taine's whole work is built about this
problem: Freud took it up in the final, theoretical

chapter of *The Interpretation of Dreams*, where he writes:

> '. . . illnesses - those, at least, which are rightly named 'functional' - do not presuppose the disintegration of the apparatus or the production of fresh splits in its interior. They are to be explained on a *dynamic* basis - by the strengthening and weakening of the various components in the interplay of forces, so many of whose effects are hidden from view while functions are normal.[16]

How close Freud came to Taine's basic conception of the life of the psyche considered as a complex equilibrium, becomes particularly clear when he writes of 'repression' or 'inhibition'. Both concepts correspond to Taine's 'reduction', the latter more closely than the former. In 'repression' an idea is violently expelled from the conscious mind, while Taine's 'reduction' simply means that it is adapted to the influence the system of mental equilibrium permits. When, a few months after having encountered Taine's work, Freud took up the notion of inhibition, it was under the influence of the idea of equilibrium. Inhibition in the development of ideas springs from a conflict between the powers of the psyche and results in a compromise between them; inhibited ideas may at times reach consciousness under the form of such a compromise.[17]

This idea, which accords nicely with Taine's dynamic conception of the psyche, reappears and is taken further in *The Interpretation of Dreams*. However it must be noted that Freud's dynamic operates on a level essentially different from that of Taine, whose doctrine - like Herbart's - is constructed in purely intellectual terms. Taine's exposition is exclusively concerned with intellectual representations; the promptings of the will, desires or sentiments, play no role whatever, and the equilibrium whose conditions he studies is that which guarantees a correct conception of reality. Taine himself was acutely aware of this deficiency; in his preface he wrote that the psychology of the intelligence must, in fact, be supplemented by a theory of the will, but that this was beyond his powers. (It must be added that his pupil, Ribot, made this his business.) As a clinical observer, Freud was in this respect better equipped. Taine's psychology is in some measure 'professorial', a doctrine of the mind appropriate to a man of theory; but Freud knew from experience that sentiments and desires play a decisive role for the generality of men. When an idea is resisted or 'reduced', the explanation - according to Taine's system - lies in its erroneous character; on the other hand, according to Freud, it represents a forbidden desire. What the two systems have in common is the conception, derived from Darwin, of the life of the psyche as a battlefield where the conflict between various tendencies is fought out; in one case this takes place in the realm of the intellect, in the other in that of the emotions and the will.

Taine's work in *De l'Intelligence* was of small significance for academic psychology. Things were quite different in the field of literature. The entire French naturalist school based themselves on Taine's work, and his theories were considered as, more or less, the last word in psychology. It is significant that, at the time of his break with the naturalist tendency, Paul Bourget should in *Le Disciple*, caricature Taine in the character of the philosopher Adrien Sixte and launch a polemical attack on his psychological theories. Ideas concerning the basic diversity of the life of the psyche, its conflicts and its dynamism, had become normative for the naturalist conception of man.

The writers who had assimilated this dramatic, associationist psychology of Taine's, set out to give these ideas form as literary documents. If we are to take Taine at his word, the arsenal of classical concepts hitherto at the disposal of writers for the description of human beings was completely outdated. It was not just that the 'faculties of the mind' had been analysed away; things stood no better with the 'characteristics' of the individual personality; even if Taine had attempted to salvage the possibility of synthetic descriptions by bringing in the concept of the *faculté maitresse*. What 'really' existed, and was consequently to be described by a truthful and realistic novelist, was the mutual conflict of the elements of consciousness.

This conception provided the initial impulse for what later became known as the 'interior monologue', and thus to a stylistic device which was, from the outset, an expression of the aims of the psycological-naturalists. The method was first intentionally employed by Edouard Dujardin in *Les Lauriers sont coupés* (1888), although comparable departures were already not unknown in naturalist writing. It is interesting that this happened only a few years before Freud began to practise 'free association' treatment with his patients, and psychoanalysis, for its part, came by degrees to inspire a succession of interior monologues in literature. There is no reason to suppose that at the time Freud knew Dujardin's book - it was none too well known - and Freud himself has said that the idea came from a humorous essay of Börne's.[18] Nevertheless the coincidence - like the associations of patients in analysis - is highly significant. Starting out from similar points of departure, similar results are arrived at. Those who had accepted the naturalist doctrine of the primal plurality of the life of the psyche must have been tempted to study this diversity more closely, in the unfolding of the imagination, only to stop short in face of the rivalry between the elements, the sudden changes, the lack of logical relations. Up to this point Freud and Dujardin were working along similar lines. But from this point on the comparison is manifestly very much to the French writer's disadvantage. His short novel may be characterized as a rather clumsily executed exercise, and it would appear that Dujardin's interest in psychology comes a good second to his delight at having hit on a new narrative resource. Freud's analysis of the processes of the psyche in himself, carried out between 1897 and 1899 and chronicled in *The Interpretation of Dreams* goes incomparably deeper; it was furthermore carried out with the aid of objective scientific controls, complemented by a theoretical underpinning of the 'minute but significant facts' which, according to Taine, research should seek to fit into their proper place.

# VII  Symbols and sexual linguistics

THERE is something else - still more important - to be considered: namely the fact that Freud's teachings, which, in their interpretation of the life of the psyche attach such great significance to the symbol, should have been developed at precisely the time when the current literary watchword was 'symbolism', at a time when writers, weary of external description, were attempting to conjure symbols out of every part of an animated reality.

If psychoanalysis had been presented as no more than a naturalist psychology of the instincts, albeit more penetrating and systematic that the rest, its significance for the literature of the twentieth century would not have become so overwhelming. From the standpoint of the historian of ideas, Freud the naturalist was somewhat behind the times. By 1900 naturalist and positivist ideas had been thrust to one side by other tendencies, not only in the field of literature but also in that of science. Even Darwinism had been obliged to put up with a reaction in biology. We need only consider the fact that Freud and Bergson were contemporaneous in laying the bases of their doctrines to conceive of the degree to which Freud was a 'retrospective contemporary' with the naturalist basis from which he operated.

It is of course true that the complex interrelations Freud unveiled in the psyche extend also to himself and his doctrine. There was about Freud something of the novelist - we have already encountered him as the enthusiastic reader of Rider Haggard's adventure story - just as in general there are various aspects of psychoanalysis which Taine would have rejected as downright fantasies. As a result Freud's ideas were all the more attractive to observers of man's being whose stock of scientific knowledge was limited - first and foremost to the poets and novelists. They were above all captivated by the role played by symbols in Freud's system. In psychoanalysis we are confronted with an unconscious conditioned by instinctive desires and primitive egoism, but this unconscious expresses itself in symbolic terms with the aid of an unwiedy, though at times truly poetic, code system. Freud himself was far from being insensible to the aesthetic character of his materials when he was engaged in his study of dreams: it was not uncommon for him to speak of a 'beautiful' dream - or something of the sort. It is by way of the faculty of image-creating, which Freud recognizes in *The Interpretation of Dreams* as belonging to the unconscious in its conflict with the 'preconscious', that the poetic elements undergo a rebirth of sorts within the framework of his, in general, radically naturalist psychology; psychoanalysis thus had a message for the literary generation that found in dreams a source for the renewal of poetry.

When, for example, the surrealists came to speak of Freud as their teacher, they did not so much have in mind his psychological system as such, but rather the perspectives it quite unexpectedly opened up for the active poetic powers dormant in man. Freud was not always in a position to go along with his self-styled followers. He wrote to Breton: 'Pleased as I am with the many signs of interest you and your friends have shown in my work, I am unable to form a clear idea of what surrealism is and of what it intends to be.'[1] But even if he preserved a quizzical attitude to most of his younger successors, it is still evident that his interest in symbols was intimately bound up with an essential element in his own being; with, if one is so inclined to put it, his literary or poetic side, which contrasts sharply with his sober and sceptical scientific exactitude.

Symbolic interpretation had already been of service to Freud as a method when he was working on hysteria; there the symptoms of illness presented themselves as the symbolic surrogates of traumatic memories. By laying bare the symbolic content of the symptoms the physician could ferret out the origin of the malady. This interpretation of symbols was only brought to perfection in *The Interpretation of Dreams*. Here (among others) is to be found the violently contested chapter in which a succession of typical sexual symbols are enumerated as if in a dictionary, along with the interpretation. What Freud has above all done is to give a detailed analysis of how symbols originate through 'condensation', 'displacement' and the visualization of 'dream thoughts'. The production of symbols is, for Freud, the essence of the 'dream work'; and he is conscious of the fact that the dream consequently realizes that which exists in popular beliefs and stories: 'Wherever neuroses make use of such disguises they are following paths along which all humanity passes in the earliest periods of civilization - paths of whose continued existence today, under the thinnest of veils, evidence is to be found in linguistic usages, superstitions and customs.'2

Tradition, supersitition, linguistic usage, memories of the childhood of humanity, dreams and poetry - all are psychologically connected. A symbolist such as Maeterlinck could not have asked for more. But although symbolism was naturally every bit as well known in Vienna as elsewhere in Europe - Hermann Bahr was its prophet there - it is not to be taken for granted that Freud therefore took an interest in it.

Symbolism was, besides, an exclusively literary preoccupation, in a way quite other than the realist and
naturalist current; Freud, on the other hand, was not a
man of letters in the sense that he applied himself to the
study of literary events: whatever came his way and
pleased him, he read assiduously, but it would appear
that none of the typically symbolist writers formed
part of his reading.

He had no need to turn to them to nourish his
interest in symbols. For him there were other sources
in plenty. Nevertheless he had one great experience in
common with the symbolist generation: the music
dramas of Richard Wagner. In a letter of 1897, to
Fliess, he tells how he had seen *Die Meistersänger*,
which had given him 'extraordinary pleasure'.[3] In the
same letter he recommended a book by the writer
Kleinpaul, on popular beliefs - one among many signs
that he was already seeking out symbols in the literature of ethnology. He discussed Greek mythology with
his friend Theodor Gompertz. He was, of course,
aware of Ibsen as a poet of symbols. But above all he
could encounter day-dreamers and creators of symbols in many spheres of the classical German literature
with which he was familiar - in the romantics and the
writers of 'Jungen Deutschland' school, in Goethe and
Conrad Ferdinand Meyer.

Freud had at all times a certain weakness for literature whose *motifs* were fantastic and romantic: his
literary tastes were far from being limited to the
naturalist current with which he had so much in common in terms of the history of ideas. On another level
of Freud's store of literary knowledge is *Don Quixote*,
a favourite since his youth. One might be inclined to
see this contrast between the fantastic and the realistic
in Cervantes as the factor which fascinated Freud; at

all events this was to become the salient point of his future work. Another notable experience was the reading of Flaubert's *La Tentation de Saint-Antoine* (1874), a work noted for its initial difficulties; Freud, however, braved these difficulties and counted himself amply rewarded for his pains.

Where literature of this sort is concerned, we may nevertheless note a certain development in Freud's intentions; he was always intensely interested in following out the complex involvements and fantastic notions to be found in such narratives, but later, as psychoanalysis took shape, more, as with dreams, with a view to finding materials for his psychoanalytic studies.

Freud read Flaubert's hallucinatory novel (or drama) not later than 1883, and the account he gave of it to his fiancée shows the extent to which he was moved. The work '. . . calls up not only the great problems of knowledge [Erkenntnis], but the real riddles of life, all the conflicts of feelings and impulses; and it confirms the awareness of our perplexity in the mysteriousness that reigns everywhere'.[4] It is only at the end of the account that the medical man speaks out and notes that one understands the book all the better if one knows that Flaubert, an epileptic, was himself subject to hallucinations.

When, fifteen years later, at the recommendation of his friend Fliess, Freud read the stories of C.F. Meyer, his reaction was quite different. There is no reason to doubt his assurances that he esteemed them highly *as literature*, and that he found the 'Hochzeit eines Mönchs' particularly 'fine'. But it is no longer a question of following in an author's footsteps and making his philosophical and psychological views one's own. Freud's newly acquired self-confidence and his therapeutic experience made it quite natural for him to consider the author as the object of psychoanalytical investigation, one among many others who would provide materials for the new theoretical edifice.

In *Gustav Adolfs Page*, the first of the 'Novelle' he read, he notes a couple of points at which Meyer's insights appear to coincide with his observations. But as soon as he comes to the second, he puts C.F. Meyer himself in the place of the patient. The Novelle now comes to be used wholly and solely as a means towards understanding the inner workings of the author's mind, and this procedure in its turn becomes a leading element in the great body of psychoanalytic doctrine. This point of view later assumes a dominant place, and Freud complained to Fliess of the lack of biographical material which might have given a firmer backing to his hypotheses.

The study of Meyer's *Die Richterin*, then, becomes the first detailed analysis of Freud's to be based on literary materials, the beginning of a genre assiduously cultivated in the psychoanalytic movement. It must be numbered among the most brilliant works of this kind; although never published, for all its shortness, it gives a succinct indication of what Freud appropriated from literature and how he interpreted it.

*Die Richterin* is a heavily fictionalized historical narrative dealing with a widow, her daughter and her stepson. As in many of the previously mentioned dramas of Ibsen, it is the revelation of an old guilt that gives rise to the catharsis at the end of the Novelle. The 'Richterin' who now rules the district with a rod of iron and administers a rigid justice has, in fact, murdered her husband; the daughter's father was, however, not her mother's husband but her lover. All this is, of course, unknown; and tragic complications threaten when the daughter and the stepson fall in love. But since it emerges in the upshot that the lovers are not, as they had thought, half-brother and half-sister, the tragedy shades off indistinctly to give place to a melodramatic ending.

The story itself is not without psychological content. The 'Richterin' attempts to 'compensate' (to use the modern term) by her rectitude and wisdom, for her guilt. But when the crime is finally revealed, the conflict within her is overcome and, in 'joyful' mood she accepts the consequences of what has happened. The struggle which has hitherto been unfolding within her is described with considerable psychological understanding. She dare not go too closely into the true relationship between the two young persons, for then 'she would have been forced to bring to light a deed buried in forgetfulness, to put to rights something that had been destroyed, to replace a link in the chain of events that she herself had snapped'.[5] Confronted with this foreboding she at once thinks in terms of a conspiracy, and when she comes face to face with her conscience, she is convinced she is dealing with an 'enemy'.

Traits such as these in the Novelle could have served as the point of departure for a deeper psychological analysis. However Freud thrust aside all such devices. He knew, as he wrote in the letter to Fliess, that C.F. Meyer had for some time been afflicted with a mental illness and that, as a young man, he had long lived with his sister. For him the subject of the Novelle was not the life of the Richterin but that of Meyer. It was he who, in his youth, had had a relationship with his sister, with which he reproached himself; and it was thus that he now diverted the guilt by portraying a brother and sister who love one another and, in reality, are not brother and sister. In the characters of *Die Richterin* he revenges himself on the 'wicked mother' who disapproved of the children's games; and that the father should be dead, Freud explains, is an expression of the commonplace wish-dream of the father's death.

Thus Freud rearranges the pieces of the puzzle, and thus he puts together another story of which the author is the subject. But he does not radically depart from the text he is interpreting. In C.F. Meyer's tale, as also in Freud's draft of an interpretation, the secret is to be found, primarily, on the psychological level; and in each case the point of departure is a wrong, or an act that is taken to be a wrong.

Here we may discern something characteristic of Freud's relationship with literature. He gladly made use of the stimuli his wide reading provided, but he transformed them in such a way as to bring them into line with his theoretical system, or in such a way that they agreed with the consulting-room data.

This is particularly true of his study of symbols. It is plain that Freud's interpretation of symbols displays a markedly 'literary' bent. In reading C.F. Meyer and others, he must in the nature of things have acquired practice in the 'reading' of symbols. Already, in *The Interpretation of Dreams*, he tells of a young man who dreamed he was climbing up a hill. At first it was difficult, but towards the end it became easier. Freud, whose task it was to interpret the dream, then and there thought of Alphonse Daudet's *Sapho* (1884), the story of a disastrous liaison between a young man and an older woman. In the novel, the young man, in the first exuberance of his love, is climbing the staircase of a house, with his beloved in his arms; passionate at first, but then ever more feeble, until he is on the point of succumbing to exhaustion - a symbolic prelude to the whole content of the book. Freud is entering, through these associations, upon the realm of eroticism, and in the unfolding of the analysis he demonstrates that his ideas are moving in the right direction. Later in the history of psychoanalysis, motifs such as 'steps' and 'stairs' are abundantly developed and, in the more recent editions of *The Interpretation of Dreams*, it is laconically stipulated that all dreams of this type signify sexual intercourse. But the initial idea would seem to come from Alphonse Daudet's novel.

Moreover Freud did not always himself have to provide the literary contribution to his dream interpretations. His patients just as frequently fulfilled this function for him. The imaginative world of the lady who had what is referred to as the 'may-beetle' dream was particularly luxuriant in literary symbols and associations. In giving a brief account of her dream she alluded, in passing, to *Die Zauberflöte* and Kleist's *Kätchen von Heilbronn*, and cited both by name. The word 'arsenic' turned her thoughts to Daudet's novel *Le Nabab* (1877), in which, in order to restore his 'vigour', the Duc de Mora obtains arsenic pills from his physician. From this dream Freud deduced that the lady in question desired a more lively conjugal activity on the part of her ageing husband.[6] But this is no more than the further development of a theme that, in Daudet, already plays a symbolic role. Arsenic stands for something that typifies Parisian 'highlife'; it makes the jaded 'insatiable for poison and for life', it creates a craving for enjoyment and a factitious youth which contrasts with the actual youth of another principal character in the book, the uncorrupted Paul de Géry.

Many other instances might be mentioned in which, in his interpretation of dreams, Freud leans for support upon literary symbols. Despite this it would be an exaggeration, in the context, to speak of anything more than momentary borrowings. These lend colour to the presentation and throw light upon an imaginative world conditioned by the times of Freud and his patients, but they in no way explain the method of dream interpretation. Freud would have been hard put to it to discover in literature a model for the decipherment of symbols and free associations that constituted *The Interpretation of Dreams.*

What is more, there are reasons to draw attention to another influence. When Freud interprets a dream, his exposition often gives the impression of a lecture on philology. The associations leap from one language to another, an individual's expressions reveal themselves to be ingenious plays on one or more - often 'difficult' - words. In Freud and some of his patients one is inclined to see a psychic process in which, at least on the surface, associations more often concern words themselves than the ideas they represent. Freud himself noted this and he emphasises how superficial the associations need to be in order to force their way into the dream:

> The ideas which transfer their intensities to each other stand in the loosest mutual relations. They are linked by associations of a kind that is scorned by our normal thinking and relegated to the use of jokes. In particular we find associations based on homonyms and verbal similarities treated as equal in value to the rest.[7]

As an example of the feats of philological artistry which, according to Freud, dreams accomplish (and which the dream interpreter must make the object of his quest), we may return to the world *norekdal*, already cited. A far more instructive case is the following, from one of Freud's own dreams:

> In a confused dream of my own of some length,
> whose central point seemed to be a sea voyage, it
> appeared that the next stopping place was called
> '*Hearsing*' and the next after that '*Fliess*'. This last
> word was the name of my friend in B[erlin], who
> has often been the goal of my travels. 'Hearsing'
> was a compound. One part of it was derived from
> the names of places on the suburban railway near
> Vienna, which so often end in 'ing'; Hietzing, Lies-
> ing, Mödling (Medelitz, '*meae deliciae*', was its
> old name - that is '*meine Freud*' ['my delight']).
> The other part was derived from the English word
> 'hearsay'. This suggested slander and established
> the dream's connection with its indifferent insti-
> gator of the previous day: a poem in the periodical
> *Fliegende Blätter* about a slanderous dwarf called
> 'Sagter Hatergesagt' ['He-says Says-he']. If the syl-
> lable 'ing' were to be added to the name 'Fliess' we
> should get 'Vlissingen', which was in fact the stop-
> ping-place on the sea voyage made by my brother
> whenever he visited us from England. But the Eng-
> lish name for Vlissingen is 'Flushing', which in
> English means 'blushing' and reminded me of the
> patients I have treated for ereutophobia, and also
> of a recent paper on that neurosis by Bechterew
> which had caused me some annoyance.[8]

At first sight, a passage such as this appears,
although only on textual grounds, to be a linguistic
excursus on proper nouns. A closer examination
reveals a Rudbeck-like richness of word associations.[9]
It is interesting, in the circumstances, that in the early
1890s Freud had studied the writings of an etymologist

whose approach to the subject of associations was very far from being narrow or quibbling. In 1897 Freud recommended Fliess to get hold of Rudolf Kleinpaul's *Die Lebendigen und die Todten in Volksglauben, Religion und Sage*, and in a note to *The Interpretation of Dreams* it is stated that Bleuler and his pupils had recourse to Kleinpaul's books in their work on symbolism.

Freud too has occasion to refer to him when he was writing *The Interpretation of Dreams*. Kleinpaul was especially well known for his etymologically-oriented works on the development of language. Like Freud - and Schopenhauer, Hartmann and Weininger - he considered himself an anti-academic scholar and he kept up a lively contestation with the academics. One of his principal works was *Die Rätsel der Sprache* (1890).[10] In it he styled himself 'word interpreter', as Freud was later to style himself 'dream interpreter', and in it he set out, in the terms that would have been employed in his time, to explore by way of etymologies, the residues of an ancient popular consciousness and pre-logical modes of thought. This among other things, is what Freud laid bare in dream-material.

When it came to bringing into prominence the sexual element in the life of the mind, Kleinpaul was one of Freud's precursors; his province was the sexual aspects of language. He had been taken to task for the 'tinge of impropriety' in his earlier books, and in the foreword to *Die Rätsel der Sprache* he retorted in a way that must have been to Freud's liking:

> Every successful word interpretation must be celebrated as a victory of Oedipus, as a masterstroke against the Sphinx of language; it is to be hymned in Thebes as a new glimpse of what lies

within, to be greeted as a new penetration of the secrets of the popular soul. In that soul the lofty and the base live in close proximity - what in the end, is the meaning of 'lofty' and 'base'? For the philosopher there is really no distinction; cold and pitiless, *oculo irretorto*, he looks with a calm clarity upon good and evil. The people are realistic: they have a sound intelligence and vigorous minds - which is in no way to say that they lack poetry. On the basis of a childlike naïveté and innocence they construct a manly, robust morality. Brute needs, powerful instincts and strong passions, the drives of nature and the genital organs dominate them - about these and about eating and drinking, as Schiller himself admits, half the world, if not the whole world, moves. The most profound myths and the most important symbols are subject to this. I do no more than recall the legends of Prometheus and of the fall of man and insist that the central part of the riddle, that which for anatomists is the determining part, should not be cut out of the body of language.[11]

This same perception was later to serve the psychoanalytically oriented researcher Hans Sperber as the basis for his work on the nature of language. Kleinpaul in his day lived up to his precepts and never missed an occasion to point out the sexual allusions in language. The catalogues he presents in this context bear a striking resemblance to the celebrated list of dream symbols that Freud gives in *The Interpretation of Dreams*, and the examples given are also in many respects similar. Kleinpaul sought, as did the psychoanalysts, to reopen the ways 'that all humanity had travelled in ancient periods of culture',[12] and chose to do this by taking the route of language, while Freud chose dreams and the imaginings of neurotics.

Both sought the secrets by a road that led them from one word to another, from one representation to another, and it is impressive to see how often they came upon comparable phenomena. Kleinpaul, the etymologist, for example, remarks on the contradictory aspect of language:

> As far as the people are concerned, one can never be sure that, at the next moment, they will not contradict themselves, that they will not make use of the same word in an entirely different sense, indeed in a sense completely contradictory to that previously employed. . . . The most extraordinary modifications present themselves, with concepts as previously with sounds, impetuous leaps and transformations, such as no one would have expected, no one would have thought possible - save the word interpreter.[13]

Freud might well have said much the same of the language of dreams. In *The Interpretation of Dreams* he states that the symbols in dreams are often ambiguous: 'As with Chinese script, the correct interpretation can only be arrived at on each occasion from the context.'[14] This characteristic trait very early aroused the displeasure of critics of psychoanalysis and led to Freud's being condemned as arbitrary. His response might properly have been that, as etymologists have demonstrated on good historical grounds, ordinary language has the same tendency to vagueness.

According to Freud's dream theory, the unconscious expresses itself with the aid of metaphors and symbols. This is likewise the case with 'the popular soul' in Kleinpaul's studies of language. At a clearly determined stage in the evolution of humanity, he held, the transfer of meanings was not effected on a basis of logical relations or out of practical considerations, but through poetic channels, by means of metaphors. Language, Kleinpaul again and again stressed, is full of metaphors which, however, draw our attention to the danger of demanding too much of allegories: a river has a mouth,[15] but that does not prevent it [at least in German] from having a 'knee' at a slightly higher point.[16] In line with the basic concepts of his linguistic doctrine, Kleinpaul takes a particular interest in every linguistic symbol connected with sexual life; and in this connection the effort to avoid direct and shameless expression serves as a stimulus to the symbol-creating fantasy: 'The sexual equipment in particular, which in all men lives its own life, very often in no sort of harmony with the total organism, seems to call forth this species of myth-formation.'[17]

In this context Kleinpaul touches on the realm of psychology. From Plato's *Republic* he cites the definition of man as a threefold being, comprising a man, a lion and a many-headed monster. Kleinpaul shares this view, and comments thus on the text: 'Man pure and simple, the truly human within man, would thus be the reasonable, philosophical essence within us which, sad to say, is inextricably bound up with another, "semi-precious", and a third, a wholly base, great wild beast, and only with difficulty masters the whole multiple organism.'[18]

This mythological image of man is not without points of contact with the doctrine of the conscious, the preconscious and the unconscious that Freud sketched for the first time in the final chapter of *The Interpretation of Dreams*. But above all his technique as a dream interpreter would appear to have been formed under the influence of Kleinpaul's quest for the symbolic residues in language. According to Freud it is characteristic of the language of dreams that it is often limited, even on crucial points, to hints, to allusions. This phenomenon is closely related to what Freud called 'displacement', that is to say the way in which the essential message of a dream often takes only a subordinate place in the manifest concatenation of dream materials. This led Freud by degrees to his researches into plays on words and jokes, set down in *Jokes and Their Relation to the Unconscious.*

When he was writing this book, Freud had Kleinpaul's *Die Rätsel der Sprache* to hand. A great many of the jokes Freud cites are drawn from this volume. But it is probable that Kleinpaul's work had already, a good deal earlier, alerted his attention to linguistic ambiguities. The first analysis of this sort to be carried out by Freud was published in 1898 under the title 'The Psychical Mechanism of Forgetting', and was concerned with explaining how it came about that Freud himself forgot the name *Signorello*. The name *Boltraffio* had taken its place in his mind, and, on analysis, the matter revealed itself to contain a series of allusions to the repressed subject of 'death and sexuality'. This corresponded pretty closely with what Kleinpaul called 'a rotten joke' [*einen schlechten Witz*],[19] as, for example, when a prince-elector is obliged to say that the doorkeeper was laid up with a fever, but will not condescend to mention so vulgar a matter and has recourse to the circumlocution *Januarius jacet in Februario.*[20] Like Freud, Kleinpaul believed in the demon that inspires printer's 'literals' - among others he quotes the story of the compositor who transposed the biblical 'Dein Wille soll deinem Manne unterworfen sein, und er soll dein Herr sein' [Thy will shall be subject unto thine husband, and he shall be thy lord] into 'Dein Wille soll deinem Manne unterworfen sein, und er soll dein Narr sein' [Thy will shall shall be subject unto thine husband, and he shall be thy buffoon].[21] It was of course perfectly clear that linguistic mishaps of this sort come about particularly frequently in the sexual domain, for that touches mankind very closely, and so must not be expressed in too explicit a manner - Freud would have said that it was subject to the 'censorship'.

# VIII   Philosophy of the unconscious

THE researches of Bernfeld and others have shown the
extent of the young Freud's debt, in his laboratory
work, to Helmholtz and his pupils Brücke and Mey-
nert. But at the same time as Freud's university
teachers were, in the 1890s, drawing away from him
and his work on hysteria and the neuroses, Freud himself was drawing away from academic learning and
finding stimulus elsewhere - in his literary discoveries
and in fundamental research that developed in opposition to the academics. Among the names to be mentioned in this connection we may count Darwin,
Taine, Brandes, Weininger and Kleinpaul. Among
them too might be counted Max Nordau; this writer,
like those already mentioned, operated in the free territory of literature and could find no words condemna-
tory enough for the dry-as-dust ideas lauded in
academic quarters. Freud took an interest in his frank
and outspoken writings, but was disappointed on meeting him in Paris - it was Max Nordau who wrote in the
'norekdal' style. In the nature of things this group also
included Nietzsche, whose contribution to Freud's
teachings was the slogan 'the transvaluation of all psychical values'.[1]

Opposition to the academics was then as salient a trait
of advanced thinking as opposition to church and
state. But radicalism too has need of traditions; and
thus the forms taken by the anti-academic movement
depend to a certain extent on the support available.
Kierkegaard's solitary and dissident personality provided the impetus for the modern breakthrough in the
Scandinavian countries; his example was perhaps
more important than the influence he exerted through

91

his ideas. Schopenhauer played a comparable role in the German-speaking countries. In the spiritual climate at the turn of the century in Germany, he was esteemed as *the* philosopher, and that not merely because he represented a naturalistic romanticism in keeping with the general situation of the epoch. He profited equally from the fact that he was taken for an adversary of everything academic; one could cite him as one's authority on matters of learning without being suspected of self-conceited donnishness. Filtering through innumerable channels - Wagner's music-drama was but the most important - his pessimistic philosophy contributed to the formation of the world of ideas and the atmosphere of the *fin de siècle*. Of all the writers we have named there is not one (other perhaps than Darwin) who was not influenced by Schopenhauer in one way or another.

The same is true, *cum grano salis*, of Freud. When, as emerges in his essay on lapses of memory, Freud discovered that his subconscious was preoccupied with the theme of sexuality and death, he might well have added that his subconscious was assuming a characteristically Schopenhauerian stance. Death and sexuality were likewise the principal *motif* in Schopenhauer's philosophy. This general kinship, particularly emphasized by Thomas Mann, need not necessarily mean that Freud had devoted himself with any great assiduity to the study of Schopenhauer's metaphysics. There is no evidence for his having done so, and in his *Autobiographical Study* Freud himself denies having read Schopenhauer before 1900. Rather he belonged to a literary current, stemming from Schopenhauer and characterized by pessimism and determinism with overtones of romanticism, and by a frank treatment of the central erotic theme. Like Hartmann and

Nietzsche, Kleinpaul and Weininger, Freud took up a position outside official science and created a species of metaphysics on a basis drawn from the natural sciences.

Thomas Mann draws attention to the parallels between the '*id*' in Freud and the 'will' in Schopenhauer; psychoanalysis, in Mann's view, reveals itself as 'a translation of the latter's metaphysics into psychology'.[2] But he found 'the most profound and mysterious point of contact' by placing Freud's writings in apposition to Schopenhauer's essay 'Transcendental Speculations on Apparent Design in the Fate of the Individual'.[3] Schopenhauer's psychology of dreams, his treatment of the sexual as 'argument and paradigm', his entire mental construct amount, in Mann's eyes, to an extraordinary anticipation of psychoanalysis.

The coincidence of ideas comes as something less of a surprise if, instead of with Schopenhauer, the comparison is made with Schopenhauer's most important disciple, Eduard von Hartmann, a writer Freud had demonstrably studied. Moreover, Freud himself has pointed out (in the notes to *The Interpretation of Dreams*) the most striking concordances with the work of this philosopher, although he would appear to imply that it was only after the event that he first met with Hartmann's work. It is perhaps correct that, in the literal sense, it was only after having written *The Interpretation of Dreams* that he engaged in an intensive study of *The Philosophy of the Unconscious*, but only in the literal sense. Hartmann's book is already cited in the first edition of *The Interpretation of Dreams*; and its author was the fashionable philosopher in Germany when psychoanalysis was taking shape. It would have been quite impossible for Freud to avoid becoming aware, in one way or another, of his ideas. Furthermore we know of one of these ways: it was through the intermediacy of Theodor Lipps, whom Freud considered the most clearheaded of the philosophers, that he came to know of the concept of the 'unconscious' which Hartmann made the pivotal point of his philosophy.

The essential difference between Schopenhauer and Hartmann lies in the fact that the latter appeals much more explicitly to science. While Schopenhauer is above all a philosopher in the romantic sense and uses his data primarily as illustrations of his ideas, Hartmann in his masterwork sets out, into the bargain, to sum up the knowledge of his epoch. His philosophy attempts to be a synthesis of the sciences. Thus his work is more concrete and more tinged with the natural sciences than that of his predecessor; thus, for example, he integrated into his system the findings of Darwinism and of hypnosis-based psychology and in general referred widely to the accepted scientific doctrines of the turn of the century.

It was Freud who, in the later editions of *The Interpretation of Dreams*, pointed out the basic agreement with Hartmann, after another writer had drawn it to his attention. As might be expected, the agreement lies in the concept of the unconscious as such. What Thomas Mann said *à propos* of Freud may equally well be said of Hartmann's philosophy, namely that in his philosophy the id (or the unconscious) occupies the greater part of the self, whilst the ego has as its domain only a small, delimited territory - 'much as Europe is a small and lively province of the greater Asia'.[4] But this idea is not in and of itself original; Hartmann and Freud share it with many others; thus, for example, Taine assures us in the celebrated

preface to *De l'Intelligence* that 'the greater part of ourselves is beyond our reach, and the visible self is
immeasurably smaller than the hidden self'.[5]

Hartmann and Freud, however, distinguish themselves from Taine by the manner in which they charac-
terize the unconscious. Whilst for Taine the
unconscious contains nothing more than disordered
associations that seek to break through into consciousness, for Hartmann, as for Freud, the unfolding of
unconscious ideas is governed by unconscious 'intentions'. In its efforts to bypass the censorship the unconscious can even make use of intelligent ruses. What we
have here, basically, is a legacy from Schopenhauer,
who held that in man, as in the rest of nature, the will
was unconscious. In the unconscious, Hartmann
wrote, will and idea ('representation') are as one - in
contradistinction to what happens in the case of conscious reflection. It is entirely possible for the conscious to think about something without willing it,
whereas for the unconscious, 'nothing can be represented that is not willed'.[6] All unconscious thinking
thus serves what Hartmann considered the primary
human instinct, that of conservation and reproduc-
tion. It is curious how, when he comes to treat of
dreams, Hartmann seems to forget this principle; the
chapter is short and, as Freud also notes in *The Interpretation of Dreams*, uninformative. He does not, of
course, go out of his way to emphasize the manifest
similarity between his own dream-theories and the sug-
gestive passages in Hartmann's philosophy.

Consequently there is as little in the way of the
'accidental' in Hartmann's conception of the unconscious as there is in Freud's. On the contrary: it is here
precisely that an inexorable, teleological determinism
governs the unfolding of the imagination. Whether in

unconscious artistic creation or in the field of 'serendip-
ity', a rigorous and predetermined uniformity, depen-
dent on 'interest' prevails. Likewise:

> ... even if one in appearance completely aban-
> dons his train of thought to accident, or if one
> abandons oneself entirely to the involuntary
> dreams of fancy, yet always other leading inter-
> ests, dominant feelings and moods prevail at one
> time rather than another, and these will always
> exert an influence on the association of ideas.[7]

Freud is similarly of the opinion that complex and
oriented processes of thinking may exist in the unconscious, and he bases his whole doctrine of dreams on
this idea. Moreover he makes it clear that Hartmann's
philosophy was a living issue for him when he was writing the first version of *The Interpretation of Dreams*.
The philosophers (we read in the first edition) who
credited the idea of a 'calculating' unconscious had run
into difficulties in explaining the function the conscious had to fill. It is hard to see how these philosophers could have been other than Schopenhauer and
Hartmann.

Freud's remark is to the point, at least as far as Hartmann is concerned. The description of the formation
of the conscious is among the most obscure passages in
*The Philosophy of the Unconscious*; but this is by no
means to say that Freud's explanation is any more
easily intelligible. It is nonetheless easy to distinguish
here one of Hartmann's *motifs*. The conscious is for
him a first step towards a liberation from the tyranny
of the will. It is in itself associated with a malaise; but it
is a bitter pill without which there is no cure. Freud's
early therapeutic conceptions, according to which the

conscious, in throwing light on the schemes of the unconscious, in itself implies the beginnings of an expiation, is clearly related to Hartmann's praise of the wisdom of the Stoics.

In his oration on the occasion of Freud's eightieth birthday, Thomas Mann expressed a fairly widely held view in declaring that Freud had beaten out his own path as an isolated *savant*, wholly independent:

> He did not know Nietzsche, scattered throughout whose pages one finds premonitory flashes of truly Freudian insight; he did not know Novalis, whose romantic-biologic fantasies so often approach astonishingly close to analytic conceptions; he did not know Kierkegaard, whom he must have found profoundly sympathetic and encouraging for the Christian zeal which urged him on to psychological extremes; and, finally, he did not know Schopenhauer, the melancholy symphonist of a philosophy of instinct, groping for change and redemption. Probably it must be so. By his unaided effort, without knowledge of previous intuitive achievement, he had methodically to follow out the line of his researches.[8]

These lines have already provoked a reply from Ernest Jones. In point of fact Freud had known all the writers mentioned by Thomas Mann - Schopenhauer, albeit, through the mediacy of Hartmann. Moreover the list of his literary reading could be extended further than has been done here. However, there is no need to heap up examples in order to demonstrate that Freud's primitive psychoanalysis may be fitted perfectly naturally, not only into a scientific-historical context but also into a general ideo-historical and literary context which we may call that of psychological naturalism. Other writers, like the philosophers, were at the same time as Freud tracking down the secrets of the mind's unconscious life. Against this background it will appear less surprising that Strindberg for example, in the course of his *Inferno* crisis, should to an extent have carried out a self-analysis - though it is described in religious and moral terms - almost at the same moment that Freud was embarking on his own analysis, which forms the basis of *The Interpretation of Dreams*.

Freud was no more unique in having his ideas than were other innovators. As regards the seeker who was his most direct model, Darwin, we now know that all the ideas set down in *The Origin of Species* had already been formulated: this holds true not only of the idea of evolution itself but also those of the struggle for life, natural selection and the reference to the breeding of domestic animals. But briefly to sketch a thought is one thing, to give that idea scientific weight is quite another. Where Darwin was alone was in bringing together all the extensive wealth of material, fathoming the problems posed and providing abundant proofs. It was the same with Freud. Without his perseverance and his intellectual energy, the Freudian revolution would never have taken place, any more than there would have been a Darwinian revolution without Darwin. The difference between the two lies in the fact that Darwin, so far as is known, had in the beginning only the intention of bringing about a revolutionary change in the field of biology. Freud, on the other hand, set out from the start to do more than make medical discoveries. His training, his reading and his interests gave him the possibility of impinging effectively on general ideas; thus his contribution has become every bit as important in the history of literature as in the history of psychotherapy.

# Notes

1 Sigmund Freud, *The Origins of Psychoanalysis. Letters, to Wilhelm Fliess, Drafts and Notes: 1887-1902*, edited by Marie Bonaparte, Anna Freud and Ernst Kris, translated by Eric Mosbacher and James Strachey (London, 1954), p. 315.

2 *The Standard Edition of the Complete Psychological Works of Sigmund Freud* (24 vols. London), vol II *Studies on Hysteria* by Josef Breuer and Sigmund Freud (1955), p. 160.

3 Freud, *Origins*, p. 162.

4 *Ibid.*, p. 156. [See also Ernest Jones, *Sigmund Freud, Life and Work* (2 vols., London, 1953), vol. I, pp. 278-9. The discrepancy between these two sources regarding the date of von Berger's review probably need not be taken very seriously. I.W.]

5 *Aristotles' Poetik* übersetzt und eingeleitet von Theodor Gompertz. Mit Einer Abhandlung: *Wahrheit und Irrtum in der Katharsistheorie des Aristotles* von Alfred Freiherrn von Berger (Leipzig, 1897).

6 See in particular Frederick J. Hoffmann, *Freudianism and the Literary Mind* (London and New York, 1959).

7 Freud, *Origins*, p. 228. [The original reads: 'So bleibt man immer ein Kind seiner Zeit, auch mit dem, was man für sein Eigenstes hält.' As Professor Brandell points out to me in a personal communication, this should properly be translated: 'So one still remains a child of one's age, even with something one *thinks* is one's very own.' I.W.]

8 Freud, *Standard Edition*, vol. II, p. xxix.

9 Jones, *op.cit.*, vol. I, pp. 189, 380.

Chapter II PSYCHOLOGICAL NATURALISM

1 Edmond and Jules de Goncourt, *Journal des Goncourts. Mémoires de la vie littéraire 1851-1895* (Paris, 1906), vol. III, 1, entry for 24 December 1888.
2 *Ibid.* vol. II, 3 (Paris, 1894), entry for 26 May 1879. [Further light is thrown on Edmond de Goncourt's attitude to Charcot by the entry for 24 December 1888, cited above, which goes on to say: 'When one comes to the point, he is a man of lowly origins, a man who will always be a student and will never manage to rise to the level of a gentleman.' I.W.]
3 *Letters of Sigmund Freud 1873-1939*, edited by Ernst L. Freud, translated by Tania and James Stern (London, 1961), p. 196.
4 Freud, *Standard Edition*, vol. III, pp. 11ff.
5 *Ibid.*, pp. 19-20.
6 Edmond and Jules de Goncourt, *Germinie Lacerteux*, avec une postface de Enzo Caramaschi (Naples and Paris, n.d. [1969]), p. 25.
7 *Ibid.*, p. 109.
8 Hans Lindström, *Hjärnornas kamp* (Uppsala, 1952), p. 154ff.
9 August Strindberg, *Samlade skrifter*, ed. J. Landquist, vol. LIV, p. 18.


Chapter III POSITIVISM AND PESSIMISM

1 Freud, *Letters*, p. 375.
2 Freud, *Origins*, p. 128.
3 J.P. Jacobsen, *Niels Lyhne*, translated by Hanna Astrup Larsen (New York, 1919), p. 160.
4 *Ibid.*
5 *Ibid.*, p. 273.
6 *Ibid.*, pp. 283.
7 *Ibid.*, p. 284.

8 Freud, *Origins*, p. 315.
9 Freud, *Letters*, p. 376. See also Erich Fromm, *Sigmund Freud's Mission* (London, 1959), pp. 71ff.
10 Freud, *Origins,* p. 286.
11 Georg Brandes, *Ferdinand Lassalle* (London, 1911), pp. 107-8.

*Chapter IV* ISOLATED IN VIENNA

1 Freud, *Letters*, p. 259.
2 Werner Kraft, Karl Kraus. *Beitrage zum Verständnis seines Werkes* (Salzburg, 1956), p. 57.
3 Freud, *Letters*, p. 260.
4 *Ibid.*
5 Jones, *Sigmund Freud*, vol. II, p. 9, quoting Phyllis Bottome, *Alfred Adler* (London, 1939), p. 90.
6 *Georg Brandes und Arthur Schnitzler. Ein Briefwechsel*, ed. G. Bergel (Berkley, Calif., 1956), p. 56.
7 *Ibid.*, p. 68.
8 *Ibid.*, p. 71.
9 *Ibid.*, p. 29.
10 Freud, *Letters*, p. 345.
11 Jones, *op.cit.*, vol. I, p. 380.
12 Arthur Schnitzler, *Gesammelte Werke* (Berlin, 1922), p. 32 (Paracelsus in Scene 7).
13 *Ibid.*, p. 57 (Cyprian in Scene 11).

*Chapter V* IBSEN AND FREUD

1 Freud, *Standard Edition*, vol. IV, p. 296.
2 *Ibid.*, vol. V, pp. 421ff.
3 *Ibid.*, vol. IV, p. 257.
4 Henrik Ibsen, *Ghosts and Other Plays*, translated by Peter Watts (Harmondsworth, 1964), p. 61 (= *Ghosts*, Act 2).

5 Halvdan Koht, *Life of Ibsen* (New York, 1971), p. 331.

6 Ernst Haeckel, *History of Creation*, translated by E. Ray Lankester (London, 1876), pp. 134-5. See also Gertrude Himmelfarb, *Darwin and the Darwinian Revolution* (London, 1959), pp. 157ff.

7 Henrik Ibsen, *Hedda Gabler and Other Plays* translated by Una Ellis-Fermor (Harmondsworth, 1976 - first published 1950), p. 136 (= *The Pillars of the Community*, Act 4).

8 Freud, *Standard Edition*, vol. II, p. 8.

9 *Ibid.*

10 *Ibid.*

11 *Ibid.*, p. 117.

12 *Ibid.*, p. 121.

13 Jakob Bernays, *Grundzüge der verlorenen Abhandlung des Aristoteles über Wirkung der Tragödie*. With an introduction by Karlfried Gründer (Hildesheim/New York, 1970), p. 28.

14 Ibsen, *The Master Builder and Other Plays*, translated by Una Ellis-Fermor (Harmondsworth, 1976 - first published 1958), p. 110 (= *Rosmersholm*, Act 4).

15 *Ibid.*, p. 119.

16 Freud, *Standard Edition*, vol. II, p. 7.

17 Ingjald Nissen, *Sjaelelige kriser i menneskets liv* (Oslo, 1931), Chapter 4.

18 Ibsen, *Hedda Gabler and Other Plays*, p. 244 (= *The Wild Duck*, Act 5).

19 Freud, *Standard Edition*, vol. XVI, p. 382.

20 Koht, *Life of Ibsen*, p. 372.

21 Ibsen, *Hedda Gabler and Other Plays*, pp. 325, 349 (= *Hedda Gabler*, Acts 2 and 3).

22 Koht, *Life of Ibsen*, p. 399.

23 Freud, *Standard Edition*, vol. II, p. 132.

24 Ragnar Vogt, *Den Freudske psykoanalyse* (Oslo, 1930), p. 75.

25 Koht, *op.cit.*, p. 388.

26 Georg Brandes, *Henrik Ibsen. Bjornstjerne Bjorn-son. Critical Studies* (London, 1899), p. 102.
27 Bertold Litzmann, *Ibsens Dramen, 1877-1900* (Hamburg/Leipzig, 1901), p. 118.
28 Koht, *op.cit.*, p. 388.
29 Ibsen, *A Doll's House and Other Plays*, translated by Peter Watts (Harmondsworth, 1965), p. 297 (= *The Lady from the Sea*, Act 4).
30 *Ibid.*, p. 300.
31 *Ibid.*
32 *Ibid.*, p. 308.
33 *Ibid.*, pp. 328-9.
34 *Ibid.*, p. 329.
35 *Ibid.*, p. 326.
36 *Ibid.*
37 Alf Kjellén, *Diktaren och havet* (Stockholm, 1957), p. 139; see also, p. 38.
38 Ibsen, *A Doll's House and Other Plays*, p. 327.
39 Freud's friend Jung was certainly fully aware of the 'psychoanalytic' trend in *The Lady from the Sea*. In an interesting passage in a communication concerning a current case of his (*The Freud-Jung Letters*, ed. W. Maguire, tr. R. Manheim and R.F.C. Hull, London, 1974, p. 92, letter of 1 October 1907), he wrote to Freud: 'Every properly analysable case has something aesthetically beautiful about it, particularly this one, which is an exact copy of Ibsen's *Lady from the Sea*. The build-up of the drama and the thickening of the plot are identical with Ibsen's ...'

*Chapter VI* MAN NATURALLY MAD

1 Freud, *Standard Edition*, vol. XVI, p. 284.
2 *Ibid.*, p. 285.
3 *Ibid.*, p. 340. See also Jones, *Sigmund Freud*, Vol. I, pp. 51ff.

4 *Ibid.*, p. 354.
5 Freud, *Standard Edition*, vol. V, p. 548.
6 *Ibid.*, p. 549.
7 Freud, *Standard Edition*, vol. V, pp. 453-4.
8 George Brandes, *Menschen und Werke* (Frankfurt a. M., 2nd ed., 1895), pp. 362-3.
9 Haeckel, *History of Creation*, (Fourth, revised, edition, London, 1892), p. 293.
10 Freud, *Origins*, p. 157.
11 Hippolyte Taine, *On Intelligence*, translated by T.D. Haye (London, 1871), p. 81.
12 *Ibid.*, pp. 70-1.
13 P.-V. Rubow, *Hippolyte Taine* (Copenhagen/Paris, 1930), pp. 102ff.
14 Taine, *op.cit.*, p.90.
15 Taine, *De l'Intelligence*, 3rd edition (Paris, 1878), p. 16. [The passage is absent from the English translation I.W.]
16 Freud, *Standard Edition*, vol. V, p. 608.
17 Freud, *Origins*, pp. 238-40, esp. p. 240.
18 Jones, *Sigmund Freud*, vol. I, pp. 270-1.

*Chapter VII*  SYMBOLS AND SEXUAL LINGUISTICS

1 See Didier Anzieu, *L'Auto-analyse* (Paris, 1959), p. 186.
2 Freud, *Standard Edition*, vol. V, p. 347.
3 Freud, *Origins*, p. 238.
4 Jones, *Sigmund Freud*, vol. I, pp. 191-2.
5 C.F. Meyer, *Sämtliche Werke*, vol. 2 (Leipzig, n.d.), p. 195.
6 Freud, *Standard Edition*, vol. IV, pp. 289ff.
7 *Ibid.*, vol. V, p. 596.
8 *Ibid*, vol. IV, p. 298.
9 [Olav Rudbeck (1660-1702), was the son of a distinguished anatomist and himself a physician (he was the first to describe the function of the

lymph-glands). The baroque exuberance of his talents was not confined to medicine; he was twice rector of Uppsala University; as an architect he designed a new anatomical institute for his *alma mater*; his linguistic speculations, which one gathers, showed as much imagination as learning, won him wide acclaim, especially *Thesauri linguarum Asiae et Europae harmonici prodromus* (Uppsala, n.d.). Imagination was prominent also in his historical studies; in *Atland eller Manheim* he took up the theories of the sixteenth-century Primate of Sweden Johannes Magnus and set out to demonstrate that Sweden was at once identical with Plato's Atlantis and the earthly paradise of the Bible. He was in addition well thought of as a botanist and typographer. I.W.]

10 [Rudolph Kleinpaul, *Die Rätsel der Sprache. Grundlinien der Wortdeutung* (Leipzig, 1890). Until the recent republication of his *Sprache ohne Worte* (Leipzig, 1888, reprinted The Hague and Paris, 1972), Kleinpaul was virtually forgotten. His reputation in his own time would seem to have been that of a 'populariser', which is rarely much of a recommendation among academics. Born in Grossgrabe 1845, he died in 1918 in Leipzig, barely three weeks before the end of the war. He pursued his university studies first in Leipzig, then in Berlin; subsequently he travelled widely, publishing several guidebooks - including, in 1881, one for Wales. He spent a good deal of time in Italy and in 1902 edited a German-Italian, Italian-German dictionary. His half-dozen or so books on linguistics for the most part appeared in the 1890s. In 1899 he published a tidy-sized monograph entitled *Wie heisst der Hund?*, devoted to the names given to dogs. I.W.]

11 *Ibid.*, p. viii.

12 See note 2 above.

13 Kleinpaul, *op.cit.*, p. 106
14 Freud, *Standard Edition*, vol. V, p. 353.
15 Kleinpaul, *op.cit.*, pp. 156f.
16 *Ibid.*, p. 158.
17 *Ibid.*, p. 163.
18 *Ibid.*, p. 164.
19 *Ibid.*, p. 309.
20 *Ibid.*, p. 314.
21 *Ibid.*, p. 316.

*Chapter VIII*  PHILOSOPHY OF THE UNCONSCIOUS

1 Freud, *Standard Edition*, vol. IV, p. 330.
2 Thomas Mann, *Essays of Three Decades*, translated by H.T. Lowe-Porter (London, n.d. [1947]), p. 417.
3 *Ibid.*, p. 418.
4 *Ibid.*, p. 417.
5 Taine, *De l'Intelligence* (3rd. ed., Paris, 1878), p. 9. The passage is absent from the English translation cited.
6 Eduard von Hartmann, *Philosophy of the Unconscious*, authorised translation by W.C. Coupland (London, 1931), three volumes in one, II, p. 55.
7 *Ibid.*, I, p. 284.
8 Mann, *op.cit.*, p. 412.

# Index